a FASTED LIFE

LIVING A LIFESTYLE OF INTIMACY
AND POWER WITH GOD

a FASTED LIFE

LIVING A LIFESTYLE OF INTIMACY
AND POWER WITH GOD

PHILIP *Renner*

FOREWORD *by* RICK RENNER

Published by Harrison House Publishers
Shippensburg, PA 17257

Cover design by Eileen Rockwell
Interior design by Terry Clifton

ISBN 13 TP: 978-1-6803-1816-6
ISBN 13 eBook: 978-1-6803-1817-3
ISBN 13 HC: 978-1-6803-1819-7
ISBN 13 LP: 978-1-6803-1818-0

For Worldwide Distribution, Printed in the U.S.A.
1 2 3 4 5 6 7 8 / 26 25 24 23 22 21

Important Notice

This book is not intended to provide medical advice or to take the place of medical advice or treatment prescribed by the reader's physician. Readers are advised to consult their own doctor or qualified health professional regarding their medical conditions before embarking upon a fast of any type or duration. Neither the publisher nor the author are responsible for any possible consequences of any action or for any person reading or following the information in this book. If readers are taking any prescription medications, they should consult with their physician and not take themselves off any medications without his or her appropriate supervision.

DEDICATION

FIRST, I THANK my Lord and Savior Jesus Christ and the Holy Spirit who gave me the strength to write this book and to document my amazing journey with Him through fasting. Holy Spirit, You guided me through all the stories and experiences in this book. God, my Father, You are my dearest Friend.

Second, I dedicate this book to my wife Ella. Often I have been misunderstood by colleagues, friends, and doctors. Many of them said that my journey in fasting was absurd. Through it all, my wife has always been there—supporting my every decision, encouraging me through all of the headaches, stomachaches, and fatigue. When I thought I could not make it, Ella was always there to give me a hug that strengthened me through it all. So many times, she has confirmed what the Holy Spirit has told me.

Ella, you are always a pillar of support to me. You are an amazing wife, mother, and best friend. So much of this book is because of you. I love you with all my heart.

CONTENTS

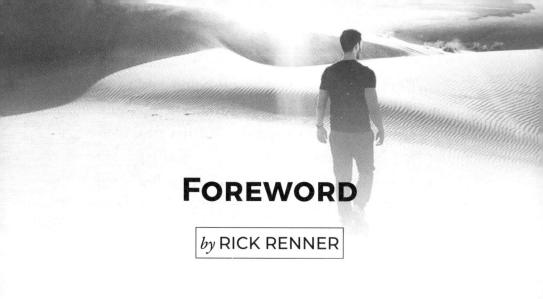

FOREWORD

by RICK RENNER

WELL, IF YOU noticed that Philip's and my last names are the same, that's because I am Philip's father. I am bringing this to your attention, because as his father, I—along with his mother, Denise—know a lot about Philip's journey into a fasted life and the fruit that it has produced.

From the very beginning, Philip always had a strong desire to be used by God. Even at a young age, he laid hands on the sick and at times prophesied over people; he loved to worship; and he had an eager heart to serve in any way possible.

One of my favorite photos of Philip is as a young eight-year-old boy in the former USSR. It was during one of the worst of times in that part of the world when life was desperate for so many people. In the photo, Philip is on his knees at the altar of one of our meetings, laying his hands on a woman who had fallen under the power of the Spirit. Philip was right there, so desperately wanting to see this woman set free in the presence of God. Even at such a young age, that was Philip—living out his dream to see God's power work mightily in people's lives.

1

Philip's great desire to know God better and to be used by Him is what led him to begin fasting when he was still a teenager. I find his journey so interesting because, at approximately the same age in my own life, I also began to spend significant amounts of time in extended fasting—which, in retrospect, I believe contributed to the growth God gave to my own ministry later in life.

In those early years, I was sowing spiritual seed that no one knew about. But God was watching, and it later produced great fruit in my life that I didn't immediately see when I was younger. In those earlier years, it wasn't uncommon for me to go on fasts that lasted 20 to 40 days. And without my ever telling Philip about that period in my life, I watched as he began to do the same thing I had done as a young man. He nearly followed the same pattern that defined my own early spiritual journey of seeking God in fasting and prayer.

Philip pressed into the Spirit with fasting because he wanted to see the power of God work in his life. In those earlier years, he began to sow spiritual seed that would produce a harvest in coming years. And Philip didn't start a practice of periodic fasting only to quit soon afterward. In the years since he first began fasting, Philip has continued to live a fasted life.

Over the years, I believe Philip has developed one of the most balanced perspectives on fasting of anyone I know. Although his approach is spiritual, it is also filled with common sense.

Much of what Philip is doing in ministry today—and what he will do in the future—is and will be a result of the precious spiritual seed he has sown as he has spent time in fasting and focused prayer. I am telling you all of this because I want you to know that what you are about to read in this book, *A Fasted Life,* is not merely rhetorical teaching. The material in this book comes directly from Philip's own life and his cultivated, balanced approach to fasting. I know it will help anyone who has a heart to seek God more intimately and to know His power more personally.

As Philip's father who has watched this process take place in his own life over the years through fasting and prayer, I have gained great respect for what he has to say on this subject. It is a subject that is important but often ignored, misunderstood, or carried out wrongly by many who have sincerely attempted to incorporate a practice of fasting into their lives.

I encourage you to carefully read this book, employing both your spirit and your mind to soak up what you read, and then to prayerfully and sensibly apply it to your own life. As you do, I am certain that you, too, will find yourself entering into the kind of fasted life that produces power and fruit for eternity.

If that is the kind of walk with God you desire, I am sure you will be helped by reading this no-nonsense guide to living a fasted life. And as you faithfully apply the truths in this book, allowing the Holy Spirit to guide you each step of the way, I believe you will begin to see eternal fruit produced in your life beyond what you can even imagine—just as has been true for the author of the pages you're about to read.

RICK RENNER
Pastor, Bible teacher, author, broadcaster

PREFACE

FASTING IS A subject that invokes strong opinions from people almost instantly. For example, some believe fasting is an exercise for those who are "super-spiritual" or a practice of those who have the time to do it. If you ask someone to miss three meals and do a water or juice fast for just one day, you will usually hear a few excuses of why "now isn't a good time" to fast. What if you suggest a fast for three days or a week, or even 40 days? You will instantly get a definite response—one that is not likely to be a positive one!

I have observed that if fasting is talked about in church at all, that discussion is generally reserved for the end of the year after all the big holiday meals as people look toward the beginning of the new year. In this instance, fasting is often viewed as one more resolution and rarely as a spiritual principle. Few messages are ever preached or taught on what fasting really is.

We have been taught that fasting is giving up Netflix, missing lunch, staying off social media for a few days, or some other act of self-denial. Although these are good behavior changes, they do not reflect what the Bible defines as fasting. It's time for today's Church to change this shallow mindset and to embrace the deeper truth of biblical fasting—a key to unlocking spiritual power, breakthrough, deliverance, health, and healing. Additionally, we must come to understand not only the act and benefit of fasting for a specific designated time frame, but also the purpose and the power of a fasted life lived in continual communion with and surrender to God.

This is why I believe the Lord has led me to write this book.

I am indebted to Jentezen Franklin, whose book on fasting stirred my heart to embark upon my first journey in fasting. His message on fasting ignited a fire within me to pursue my own experience with God through fasting and to receive the revelation insights and understanding that changed my life and resulted in this book. Within these pages, I offer you both practical and spiritual insights that are confirmed both scripturally and scientifically. I invite you to make the decision to allow your thoughts about fasting to come into alignment with God's intent about this practice.

As you come to understand the great value of fasting and prayer, I believe you will develop a new mindset that will bring you into deeper fellowship with God. A lifestyle of prayer and fasting produces ongoing communion with the Father that will keep you filled to overflowing with Him. As a result, the freshness of His presence in your life will make Him known to the world around you. That is the beauty and the power of a fasted life.

INTRODUCTION

IN THIS BOOK, I want to share with you what the Lord has taught me about fasting—and even more, about living a fasted lifestyle. The Lord has shown me that the latter develops an ongoing hunger for God even more than periods of fasting. And He is continuing to teach me. Without exception, each time I have yielded to the Lord for a time of fasting and prayer, I have emerged with a fresh impartation of His grace and power.

Let me be clear from the beginning: Living a fasted lifestyle doesn't mean that you're always on a long fast. That isn't true, and it isn't necessary. God's leading in this area will be different for each person. Listen for His prompting and then follow His way for you. I share my testimony and my examples because that's what I have experienced. But my personal examples are not the only ways to fast. Even when I fast, it is different each time.

Kenneth E. Hagin shared that the Lord told him only to fast for three days—that this would be sufficient time for him to silence his flesh and to hear from God. Brother Hagin said the Lord also told him that He would rather that he lived a fasted life. In other words, to live a lifestyle of walking in continual consecration, never eating as much as you desire, maintains the discipline of always keeping a form of restraint on fleshly appetites. Others recommend missing a meal or even intermittent fasting. The point is this: Humility, obedience, and spiritual hunger for God's Word and His ways are the common denominators of a fasted life that cultivate a lifestyle of intimacy and power with God.

This book is by no means an exhaustive study on the topic of fasting and prayer. It is, however, a very personal study drawn from my journey that shares revelation insights I gained about the value of a practice that has been misunderstood and very often neglected.

I will present examples of men and women in the Bible who fasted, as well as examples from my own scriptural experiences. As you read these accounts, I believe you will see that fasting and prayer are not only beneficial practices but also powerful, vital spiritual weapons in the arsenal of believers—especially in this hour before the Lord returns.

May I pray for you before we begin?

> *I ask the Holy Spirit to open your heart and understanding and to help you recognize the value of prayer and fasting in walking out the destiny He has planned for you. I ask Him to reveal to you your true identity as a son or daughter of God so you can enjoy fellowship with the Father and enter into partnership with Him through prayer and fasting. In Jesus' name. Amen.*

CHAPTER 1

MY JOURNEY IN FASTING

I REMEMBER WHEN I was a young boy watching how my mom would fast. We would be sitting at the dinner table and I'd ask Mom, "Why aren't you eating?" Her reply would be a simple "I'm fasting." (Note: Mom was teaching me a biblical principle, not bragging about her fast.)

At the age of ten, I didn't really understand what Mom's answer really meant, so I just thought fasting was weird. I had the idea that she was super-spiritual and that fasting was something super-hard to understand. I often wondered what happened in the room when she shut her door to pray. What encounters with God was she experiencing?

Although I still thought fasting was for the super-spiritual, I realized that there was something special that happened with God when a person fasted, because when my mom would finally come out of her room after reading and praying during her fast, there was just something different about her. To me, fasting was mysterious—but there was something beautiful about that mystery.

I remember a time when I asked Mom, "What is fasting?"

She simply replied, "Instead of eating food, I spend time with God. Time with God is more important than food."

I still thought fasting seemed weird, but something intrigued me about the idea. Of course, now I know the Holy Spirit was drawing me. I put that thought about "loving God more than food" on the shelf, believing that one day when I was older, I'd come back to it and then I'd be "super-spiritual" too.

REVIVAL IS SUSTAINED BY THE WORD

When I was 13 years old, I remember a little revival we had in the youth band at Moscow Good News Church. God started moving in our services. During worship in those youth services, I'd fall on my face in God's presence and just lie there.

Those services were really the first time I felt the tangible presence of God. He was doing something powerful, but it seemed to me it had a lot to do with the worship band. When they played, Heaven would fall down!

I wanted to be closer to that presence, so I joined the worship team. I couldn't play any instrument, and I could barely sing, but I definitely had a merry heart and a desire to be close to God. That was it.

I remember coming to rehearsal and, to my surprise, the same presence that was in the room at youth service was there at rehearsal. It was so powerful to me. Then the realization hit me: They're not rehearsing—they're worshiping! I found myself on the floor, crying out to God, "Lord, use me! Show me what You want me to do with my life!"

I cried so much during one rehearsal that I actually lost my contact lenses. The presence of God seemed to grow thicker and thicker at every rehearsal. As the band would rehearse, people who were walking around in other parts of the church would be drawn to the presence of God filling the room where we conducted rehearsal. They would worship with us and call their friends to sit in rehearsal as well.

Within a couple of weeks, it seemed like we had 20 extra people who would just come to worship with us, although they had nothing to do with the worship team. God was moving in the worship team. New songs and new sounds were arising, and it was causing a spiritual chain reaction to unfold.

I remember when the news of the anointing on the youth services and youth worship team rehearsals reached the ears of our pastor, Rick Renner. I'm the pastor's son, but I didn't say, "Dad, come to youth service—it's awesome!" Other people were talking about it, so Dad decided to sit in on a service. He felt the tangible presence of God just as everyone else did in the room.

After service Dad sat us all down to talk to us. I remember him saying, "The presence of God in this room is so powerful! It's wonderful to see you all experiencing the presence of God is such a tangible way, but I am cautious about some things happening here."

We all looked puzzled but were very attentive to hear his next words. He said, "The presence of God is strong here, but it lacks foundation. Your worship must be built on the foundation of the Word of God. You need to be singing lyrics based on the Word of God."

Then Dad asked the team if they were reading their Bibles. Most of them said no! He went on to say, "You can't grow in the Lord by living off an experience. Your life has to be built on the Word. The presence of God at your services and rehearsal was wonderful, but it will be short-lived if you don't start building it on the Word."

Dad was prophesying! The team continued to live off a feeling in God rather than the Word of God. Eventually the sense of His tangible presence began to grow less and less every service, until finally it seemed like the presence of the Lord was completely gone. I thought what had happened to our worship team was terrible, and it caused me to put a lot of attention on the Word of God. In my personal time with the Lord, I began to study the Bible more than ever before.

This whole experience put a reverent fear of God inside of me. I understood that the Word of God must be a top priority in my life.

My First Fast

By age 14, I was reading my Bible every day. I was taking notes, and I even had a notepad that had sermons in it. I felt like I was growing in God stronger than ever. One day when I was just going about my activities, I heard God say to my heart, *"It's time to fast."* I was surprised, but I knew God's voice.

As a family, we practiced hearing God's voice. We would pray all together and then sit in total silence. Finally, Dad would ask each of us, "What did God say to you?" Then we would go around the table sharing what He had spoken to our hearts.

As a result of this practice, I had learned to hear and recognize God's voice. So when I heard Him say, "It's time to fast," I knew that was the Lord. So I asked Him, "Fast for how long?" He replied, "Seven days on juices and water."

It felt like the biggest assignment ever had just been thrown on my shoulders. But I knew I had to obey, so I started my fast the next day.

I remember the horror I felt. Everyone around me at the table was eating. They would ask, "Aren't you going to eat today?"

I answered, "No, I'm fasting."

I felt like no one understood me. My brothers did not get it! My dad just said, "Okay." The person who cooked and helped take care of us told me how bad it was for a boy of my age not to eat. She said, "You are a growing boy! You need nutrients and protein!"

The only person who smiled when I said I was fasting was Mom. She said, "That's wonderful, Son!"

Then came the common question: "What are you fasting for?" Everyone in the family asked me that question. Later it felt like all my friends and the entire youth group was asking me that same question.

My reply was always, "I don't know. All I know is God told me to fast! I don't have a reason. I don't know what to pray for. I just know the Lord said to fast."

I didn't know much at all about fasting, but I knew that fasting was not starvation and that it was loving God more than food. So instead of eating, I spent time in the Word of

God. From my experience in the worship team, I knew my fasting could not be based on emotions. It had to be established on the Word of God. The Word would be my strength.

That week of my first fast felt like the longest week of my teenage years. I was so hungry! So I spent a lot of time in prayer and in reading the Bible. I always felt stronger afterward. But I was counting the seconds for that week to be over. Finally, the end of the week arrived and my fast came to an end. Having no experience in fasting whatsoever, I ate everything I got my hands on!

The first thing I ate was a stack of chocolate banana pancakes. They were so delicious; I don't even know how many I ate! Then I ate an entire pizza! Then I had some chicken, and when I arrived home I ate an entire carton of cereal. After all that, I thought I probably needed to eat something healthy, so I ate a salad with chicken. I ate so much that my stomach finally felt as a hard as a brick. I was in pain! Suddenly I had a thought: *Perhaps I overdid it a little and ate a bit too much.*

I obviously didn't know anything about fasting. I had no idea that you need to come off a fast gradually. After eating like a pig, I had to lie down because I felt horrible. But regardless of how bad I felt physically, I knew there had been a shift spiritually. I could tell that something was accomplished in the Spirit. In the natural, I had a horrible stomachache, but in the Spirit I had a sense of victory!

As you fast, you will discover that many times in the natural, situations may look pretty bad; yet in the Spirit, things will have already shifted!

My dad and mom were on a trip at the time, so the next day Mom called me to ask how it went for me as I was coming out of my fast. I told her it went well—that my stomach hurt a little bit, but I was fine. I didn't want her to know that it was the worst stomachache I'd ever had in my life and that I still felt bad the next day.

As Mom continued to talk with me on the phone, she said, "Philip, I think your fasting did something!"

"Really? What was it?" I asked.

Mom replied, "Your dad had been struggling with making a decision, but yesterday he announced that we are leaving Latvia and moving to Moscow. He said that a boldness just came on him! Philip, I think this is the result of your fast."

I was shocked but overwhelmed with joy inside. I felt as though I had accomplished something in the Spirit. I concluded from this experience that fasting is powerful. Although that fast was the hardest thing I had ever done, afterward I felt closer to God—and personally I felt like a champion. It was then and there that I realized fasting was a powerful tool in the Spirit. I was determined to learn more about it.

THE REVELATION RESURFACES

Ten years after that experience with my first fast, I was the youth pastor in our church in Moscow, Russia. I had 30 teenagers attending my youth group, and I was so excited. I loved every one of them. They were constantly hanging out in our apartment.

My wife Ella and I did all kinds of activities for the youth. Regular youth activities included picnics, prayer meetings, all-night gatherings, special events at service, concerts, and many counseling sessions. Ella and I poured our hearts into the youth ministry.

I would regularly spend four to five hours preparing for a message. But sadly, whenever I preached, the youth would laugh at me because my Russian wasn't the best at that time. It seemed like no one would remember the message. They'd just remember the embarrassing mistakes I'd make speaking Russian.

I loved the youth and everything about youth ministry, but the youth didn't like me. Out of 30 youth, I would say half of them gossiped about me behind my back—and most of those were the leaders.

I honestly didn't understand what was going on. As time went by, I grew more and more discouraged. Finally, I made the decision that I was going to give up. In three years, I'd seen only one person get saved. It seemed as though I was pouring my life into something that was producing zero results. My dad would say to me, "You're not building the youth ministry; the youth ministry is building you!"

I held on to that word as much as I could, but it came to a point when I knew I couldn't hold on any longer. The situation with the youth group and leaders had continued to spiral downward, and I was desperate for a breakthrough!

I prayed, "Lord, I have entertained them, loved them, and counseled them, yet none of it is working. What should I do ?" In that moment, I remembered how Mom would shut her door to pray as we ate at the dinner table. I recalled how she told me that fasting is powerful and that fasting means you love God more than food.

I began to study the Scriptures and found that fasting and praying was a powerful combination that caused breakthrough! So I told myself, That's it! I'm going to fast! I started with a three-day fast.

It's important to note that when you start fasting, you should only fast for the amount of time that you have faith for and is reasonable. For example, never attempt a long fast if you have never completed some short ones. Also, consult your doctor before you go on a long fast, especially if you have any underlying health conditions or are taking medications.

I decided to fast on Sundays, because I didn't want my strength to come from me at youth service; I wanted my strength to come from the Lord. I knew that if we had a good service, it would not be because of my strength, because I had none. It would be because of Jesus and Him only.

After youth service on Sundays, we always prepared food so that the youth could fellowship. Normally, I would be eating with them, but they noticed I wasn't eating. When they asked me why, I told them I was fasting. They didn't understand it and just thought I was weird. (Please understand that I was immature at that point. It is not biblical to announce one's fast; that is pride.)

I expected the youth to be impressed and to say, "That's awesome, Pastor! Go for it!" Unfortunately, that was not the case. Instead, they just responded with jokes and more talking behind my back.

I was determined I would not give up fasting to see a breakthrough. Instead, I decided to increase my commitment! So I decided to fast for one week; then I fasted for ten days. Finally, I fasted for two weeks.

With every fast, my desire to fast increased. Yet the young people's jokes and ridicule behind my back also increased. Not only was I the horrible preacher because I couldn't speak Russian well, I was the preacher who would not eat— the weird youth pastor!

It seemed like things were getting worse, not better. I was becoming more discouraged with each passing day. I needed a touch from Heaven. I knew I needed to get away from everything to hear God's voice, so my wife and I went on a little vacation together. We decided to go to Ella's grandmother's house, which was in Ukraine.

Grandma was a strong intercessor. She was also very prophetic. She had prophesied that Ella and I would be married at a time when we weren't dating or even interested in each other. In fact, we couldn't stand each other because we were so different! Grandma also knew by the Spirit which people in the leadership of the church would be faithful and who would not.

Grandma would tell Ella and me, "That person in leadership is dangerous. I'm praying against the enemy's strategies."

We would say, "Grandma, that person is awesome, well-trusted, and very strong."

But then through a chain of events, the true story would be revealed. Grandma was always right. She was always in prayer; that was her life. She worked her garden, cooked, and prayed. She was an intercessor.

I knew that if God was going to speak to me, it would be when we would go to visit Grandma in Ukraine. I knew there would be a night while we were there when I'd say good-bye to Grandma and Ella and go just spend time alone with the Lord.

Now, throughout this whole season, I was reading Jentezen Franklin's book *Fasting and Praying.* That book ignited a fire within me and started me on my fasting journey.

While reading that book and praying, I told the Lord, "Okay, God. The youth ministry is not growing. They don't even like me! The leadership team gossips behind my back. Maybe I'm not the right guy, so I'm ready to lay it down. Show me who You want to take it. The youth like it when I sing, so maybe I should just be a worship leader and forget about being a pastor."

In that moment, it wasn't that I wanted to give up on being the youth pastor; it was that I was really ready for whatever change needed to take place. In my heart, I thought if I wasn't the right person, I just wanted God to show me who was so I could step aside for that person to step into the position.

I had humbled myself before the Lord. I had searched and emptied my heart of all selfish ambition. I was no longer asking God to make the youth like me; I just wanted Him to bring the person who was best for them. Through times of prayer and fasting and spending time with the Lord in His Word, my motives had changed and I didn't even realize I was finally desiring only God's will to be done His way—for His glory and for their blessing.

I waited in silence for the Lord's reply. Finally, I picked up a pen and began to write the Lord's answer as He spoke to my heart: "No, you're not finished yet! You are pregnant! There is a generation on the inside of you. It's time to give birth!"

I was shocked. I had never heard the words "you're pregnant" in that context. I wasn't familiar with that kind of terminology in a spiritual sense, but I knew that God was speaking to me.

So I timidly asked, "How do I give birth to it?"

God answered, "Fast for 40 days."

I did not like what I had just heard. I wanted to say, "I rebuke you, Satan!" But I knew it was the Lord. My flesh was screaming, "No!" I thought to myself, *I'm not Jesus. I'm not Moses! This can't be. I have never seen anyone fast for 40 days!* Even the most spiritual people I knew had only done a 21-day fast.

I was freaked out! Still in shock, I told the Lord: "Here's our deal: If my wife agrees to my fasting for 40 days, then I will do it."

I came home that night and told Ella what had happened; then I asked her the big question: "Should I fast 40 days?" She didn't even hesitate with her reply: "If that's what the Lord told you to do, than you should do it."

I was so angry—that was not the response my flesh wanted to hear from her! I wanted her to question my decision and to give me excuses why I should not fast. I wanted her to say, "Are you sure you should do that? It will be too hard physically. This will be hard on the family because I enjoy eating with you. Meals together are a part of our fellowship, and if you fasted, that fellowship time would be gone."

That's what I wanted to hear Ella say, but her response was simply that I should do what God had told me to do. Then she asked me. "When do you start?"

I had the answer because God had already told me. I had my assignment, but I was scared. I knew that the youth already thought I was a freak when I fasted for just a week. What would they think when I fasted for 40 days?

Now, I know that as believers we have to be free of the opinion of man, because the only opinion that should matter to us is that of the King of kings. He alone is Lord. But back then I was afraid of everyone's opinion. The truth is, I was codependent and didn't know it.

I wondered what my family would think. In general, they really didn't understand why I would fast for that length of time, but they said go for it. My mom hid her response not out of fear and uncertainty, but in faith she said, "Go for it, Son!" I could tell Mom was concerned about my health in the process, but she didn't v oice her apprehension. The group opinion was, "I don't get it, but go for it."

That was all I needed. I had a word from the Lord to fast, and I had a time frame to do it. So I focused and got to it. I didn't know it at the time, but this one particular fast would change my life and cause fasting to become a lifestyle for me. Through this one act of obedience, everything in my life was about to change! Almost every year since then, I have continued this habit and discipline with the Lord.

You might not be called to commit to a 40-day fast. But a foundation needs to be established in your life to see breakthrough take place as the result of fasting as the Holy Spirit leads, whether it's a one-day, a three-day, or an even longer fast.

My "Make or Break" Moment

I can look through the years and see fruit from every fast that launched a different season in my life. Through it all, God proved that He is faithful, and He is an excellent Teacher. Let me share some of what the Lord taught me in that first 40-day fast.

I was following the Lord's specific instruction to me, which was to fast 40 days and to "give birth" to the generation inside of me. All I knew to do was to draw near to Him and give myself to consuming His Word while yielding myself to Him in prayer and in worship.

During this particular fast, an idea began to take form in my heart that I continued to pray over. The idea was to end our approach to youth ministry as something separate and to make it simply a service conducted for the youth and run by the youth with their type of format as the youth would do it—but anyone could attend. We already had three services at Moscow Good News Church each Sunday, so this youth service would be the fourth.

The more I prayed, the stronger and clearer this idea became to me. I shared my thoughts about it with my father, and we discussed it. I told him that I had been praying and fasting about it. He knew it was not an idea that I had just come up with on my own. I had prayed and fasted, holding it before God.

So my dad responded, "All right. If you believe you have a word from the Lord, go for it. This will either make or break the youth ministry, and you'll have to live with the consequences."

I said, "Okay." I was ready to do that because I knew I had heard from the Lord.

When the day arrived, I was a little nervous. After rehearsal, I walked down the hall ten minutes before I was to conduct our first youth service in this new direction. When I entered the sanctuary, there were five grandmothers sitting on the first row. That was it—no youth, just five grandmothers.

I thought to myself, *Oh, no, I've turned the youth ministry into the senior-citizen ministry!*

I turned around and went to the green room. I was so angry, because I thought I had missed it. I was even beginning to think that my 40-day fast meant nothing. Balling my hand up into a fist, I was about to hit the wall—when suddenly I thought, *No, that will hurt!* So I positioned a pillow on the couch, preparing to pound it as hard as I could—not once but multiple times.

As I was about to land my first blow, less than an inch from the pillow, I heard in my spirit: Moses was told to speak to the rock, but he hit the rock instead—and because of that, he didn't walk into the Promised Land. If you hit that pillow, you will not walk into your promised land.

Immediately I repented. I lowered my hand, and I didn't hit the pillow; instead, I fell on my knees and worshiped.

I said, "God, I love You. I don't care if there are 50 grand-mothers out there, I love You. I trust You."

When I got up and walked into the sanctuary, there were 150 people there—youth and grandmothers! And through-out the weeks and months that followed, the majority in attendance were youth, with just a few older folk mixed in.

It's so important not to give up and quit believing—no matter what it looks like! When I saw only five grandmothers sitting there ten minutes before youth service, I was tempted to think my praying was in vain. I was about to act like Peter. He stepped out of the boat onto the water and was so close to walking on the water all the way to Jesus. But, discouraged by what he saw and felt, Peter didn't make it.

But God is so faithful. He helped me, and I worshiped through to the other side.

That moment when I repented for my anger and discour-agement, falling to my knees in worship, was the "make or break moment" for me. It wasn't the youth ministry that this new idea was going to make or break—it was me.

Later I remembered that my dad had always told me, "You aren't building the youth ministry; the youth ministry is building you."

The Lord taught me an important lesson in that situa-tion. During the fast and even afterward, He was leading me into humility, removing impurities from my character, and keeping me from self-sabotage so He could fulfill His prom-ise to me. An immature, undisciplined outburst of anger cost Moses the Promised Land. A similar outburst could have cost me greatly as well.

Know this: Whenever you come before God and pour out your heart to Him in fasting and prayer, allowing Him to work change in you, that sacrifice is never in vain.

This was the first time the Lord instructed me to fast for 40 days. After that fast, the youth ministry grew from 30 to 150 youth! All the youth leaders who were against me left, and God brought in a completely new leadership team who helped me in the years that followed.

But looking back on that first fast, I realize that it wasn't even about praying and fasting for the youth. The significance of that fast was for me to gain a truly consecrated heart.

It wasn't the fast itself that produced these changes. Fasting became the dedicated occasion for me to set my focus intently on God to hear His direction, to receive His correction, and to yield myself more fully to the Holy Spirit. That consecration and obedience is what paved the way for God to move as He desired in my situation.

God is no respecter or persons. What He did for me, He will do for you. If you will choose to honor Him with time and consecration through love-directed, God-focused fasting, you will give the Lord access to demonstrate His faithfulness in your life. And in that process, He will lift off the limits that have hindered you in the past as He shifts you to another level in your walk with Him.

CHAPTER 2

BREAKING MISCONCEPTIONS: WHAT FASTING IS AND IS NOT

BEFORE WE FULLY discuss what fasting is, I think it is important to define what fasting is *not*. Fasting is not starvation. Fasting is not a diet. Although there is proven science that fasting does benefit your health, the purpose of biblical fasting is not to lose weight, although that can be a benefit. Instead, Bible fasting helps you cultivate a humble mental and emotional state to lay aside sins and weights that can shackle the heart and mind.

It may sound simple, but although biblical fasting deals with the physical, it is not focused on the physical but rather on the spiritual. It is a commitment of time in prayer and study of God's Word instead of eating.

Just think about it: If you were to add up all the time you spend on food, how much time would that be? If you include lunch meetings, coffee breaks, and food preparation for the day, I would say that you probably spend at least three hours of your day on food. Just imagine what would happen

27

with your spiritual life if you spent that time in prayer and in the study of God's Word? You would grow in God like never before.

The American or Western mindset seems to celebrate an addiction to food by using it as entertainment. Mindless snacking can also become a way to cope with stress or alleviate boredom. This misuse of food creates an unhealthy interaction with it and an attachment to food that can take on a demanding personality of its own. If you don't believe me, miss three consecutive meals and see just how much your flesh will scream, demanding food even when you know you aren't actually hungry! Fasting helps us break this addiction.

At a workshop I conducted on fasting, a young man walked up to me and said, "Fasting is so hard. I feel hungry, angry, and tired the entire time!"

My first question to that young man was, "How much time are you devoting to prayer and the study of God's Word when you fast?"

"Not a lot," he replied.

"Well then, that explains it," I said. "You aren't fasting—you are starving yourself."

I continued to explain to him that every time I feel hunger, discomfort, or fatigue during a fast, I consider it a signal for me to pray. I will then go into my room and shut the door to spend a couple of hours with the Lord in His Word and prayer. I always come out of that time feeling stronger and more energetic than I was before.

True fasting takes place when prayer, study of the Word, and time spent with the Lord become your literal source of energy.

The Hebrew word for *fasting* is *tsum*, which means "to abstain from food or to fast." In Hebrew, to fast means to shut your mouth and not allow anything to go in it.

True fasting, then, means to abstain from food and to not put anything in your mouth. Therefore, if you abstain from other things such as games, TV, social media, friends, sports, or anything else other than food, that is not fasting; that's self-discipline—which, honestly, we should practice every day.

IMPORTANT GUIDELINES IN FASTING

There are 15 spiritual precepts for fasting that I want to present for your consideration so you can invite the Holy Spirit to speak with you about their application in your own life.

Fasting and praying as a lifestyle before God is a very personal expression of worship offered from each individual to the Father. Therefore, although a precept is a principle intended to regulate behavior or thought, these are not formulas or a set of hard rules. Instead, these precepts are guidelines that can inspire heart changes and new expectations, resulting in changed behavior and mindsets. As a result, you will be able to enter deeper fellowship with the Lord through a lifestyle of fasting and prayer, which is a fasted life.

These 15 precepts of fasting as I have outlined them are as follows:

1. To abstain from TV, movies, or social media for a period is *not* fasting but behavior modification.

2. To fast should never be required or forced. Fasting is a form of worship offered to bless and honor God in a spirit of grace, not legalism.

3. To fast and pray will bring clarity that reveals God's plan for your life.

4. To fast helps silence the voice of the flesh, enabling you to hear the voice of God within your spirit more clearly.

5. To submit to God through fasting will replace pride with humility.

6. To fast releases physical healing into our bodies and equips us to handle pressure and stress.

7. The motivation of biblical fasting is to seek God's heart in consecration, not just to seek His hand as a consumer.

8. To fast doesn't change or move God. Fasting and prayer changes you to align with His will.

9. God sees you as a valuable son or daughter in His family.

10. Be astonished and astounded at what God can do through your fasted lifestyle.

11. Fasting will transform you to grow in God's love and to develop a heart of compassion.

12. Fasting done with a wrong motive is pointless and will not produce the needed results.

13. New levels of righteousness will rise and be established in your personal, daily experience as fasting gives you a God-perspective to change.

14. Fasting and prayer will birth the next generation called into ministry.

15. To break a fast correctly requires self-discipline but reaps many blessings to your spirit, soul, and body.

These guiding principles will help you stay focused and on track with your motives and expectations as you minister to the Lord in fasting. Please note—none of these precepts address any sort of regulation regarding *how long* or *in what manner* you are to fast. All of that and more is between you and the Lord. The main thing is for you to present yourself to Him as a living sacrifice with a sincere heart. The Lord will direct you as He desires from that point forward.

Fasting Is Not Behavior Modification

Although behavior modification is a good thing, it is not fasting. You can benefit from abstaining from movies, television, or social media for a season. In fact, I recommend it as a means to clear your mind of needless clutter and to calm and cleanse your own soul from unprofitable influences. But to fast is to abstain from foods. Fasting is a powerful spiritual exercise that changed my life, and I believe fasting can change your life as well.

Fasting will enable you to humble your heart before the Lord so you can come into agreement with God and into alignment with His will. Here's some practical advice: It is easier to fast evening to evening than to start a fast in the morning and end it the next morning. Just think about it: For that 24 hours, you are spending time with God instead of eating. During that time period, you are in a constant state of humility before God—and He loves the humble. Proverbs 3:34 (NLT) says, "The Lord mocks the mockers but is gracious to the humble."

Fasting is the opposite of being prideful. To fast and pray does not push your own agenda; fasting helps you align with God's agenda. When you align yourself with His will, Satan has no foothold in your life.

The only power that the enemy has over your life is the authority that you give to him. All authority in Heaven and earth belongs to Jesus (*see* Matt. 28:16). If all authority belongs to Jesus, that means Satan has none, because Jesus disarmed him of everything. As Colossians 2:15 (NLT) states, "In this way, he disarmed the spiritual rulers and authorities. He shamed them publicly by his victory over them on the cross."

So let's look at the facts:

1. Jesus stripped Satan of all his authority.

2. Christ's resurrection power is on the inside of you.

3. Fasting /humility aligns you with God's plan and power so you can live a life of victory.

I challenge you to make the choice today to take your relationship with God to the next level. He wants you to draw near to Him. If this chapter has touched your heart, it could be the Holy Spirit speaking to your heart to draw closer to Him. He wants to communicate with you on a more intimate level. He is both inviting and challenging you to draw near.

What Does Fasting Accomplish?

In Romans 12:1 (TPT), we find the perfect description of what fasting and prayer accomplish in our lives:

> *Beloved friends, what should be our proper response to God's marvelous mercies? To surrender yourselves to God to be his sacred, living sacrifices. And live in holiness, experiencing all that delights his heart. For this becomes your genuine expression of worship.*

The first words I want you to focus on in this scripture are *living sacrifices*. This scripture is usually used to explain the act of crucifying your sin nature, and that is correct. But I want us to consider a different aspect of this scripture that has become a revelation for my life.

Whenever I read the phrase living sacrifice, I think of the times I have presented my body as a sacrificial offering to the Lord in fasting. I may have felt pain in my stomach from hunger, but that was part of my sacrifice.

I remember how it felt to be cold in the middle of summer because I hadn't eaten in several weeks. This happens because our body cannot heat itself without calories from food. We truly do not realize how much food warms our bodies until we go without it for a while.

It has been in those periods of fasting that I believe I became a living sacrifice as I chose to deprive myself of food so I could devote my time and attention to the Lord. I deliberately chose to resist my need for food in order to yield to His desire for fellowship with me.

I remember going into my room and shutting the door feeling weak, only to come out strengthened by the Word and the presence of God. I chose as an act of my will to hold myself on the altar of sacrifice to the Lord through fasting. As I offered myself to Him as a living sacrifice, He truly became the Strength of my life.

So, when I see the phrase "living sacrifice," I automatically think *fasting and praying.* Why is it important to be a living sacrifice? To offer one's self as a living sacrifice is important because it is a choice to humble oneself before God.

Being a living sacrifice is an act of humility and selflessness that acknowledges God, His Word, and His ways as first and most important. It adopts a posture of humility that honors God. As we empty ourselves of self-focus, we make room to be filled with more of God. According to James 4:6, God opposes the proud and self-absorbed, but He gives grace and shows favor to the humble.

I like to think of God's favor as the moment when we turn toward Him to be a living sacrifice to Him. In that moment, God turns His face toward us, releasing the brightness of His grace and favor into our lives, and the light of His countenance rests upon us.

The next word that I want to focus on is holiness. There is no doubt in my mind that a standard of righteousness rises within us when we fast and pray. This happens because we are spending time with our righteous Father.

Through salvation, we are made partakers of His divine nature, which is righteousness. But we must cultivate an awareness of it if we are to truly walk in it. The more time we spend with the Father, the more His nature is revealed to us. And the more His nature is developed within us, the more His righteousness will be revealed through our words and actions. We feed and fortify the nature of God within us through time in His Word, His presence, and in prayer.

I remember when I first started fasting! Within about a week, I was shocked by how the things of world were not enjoyable to me anymore. I didn't want to watch TV. Even fellowship with my friends was not as satisfying. Their jokes and the thoughts and ideas that were brought to mind by what they said and did were actually distasteful to me. If I agreed to hang out with them, it was as if I had to force myself to do it.

I really didn't have a desire to hang out with friends when I could be learning from the Holy Spirit and spending time with the King of kings and the Lord of lords. All I could feel was this constant pull back into the presence of God.

The more time I spent in fasting and prayer, the more I longed for the purity and sweetness of God's presence. Nothing else could satisfy my heart anymore. In fact, what I once enjoyed or perhaps was able just to ignore began to grieve me. People shouting! Watching television! It all grieved me!

Even commercials that didn't have blatant sin in them grieved me. I would think to myself, *Why did that commercial grieve me? Why couldn't I watch it? It only had just a hint of sin!* Then I would hear the Holy Spirit speak to me and say, "The closer you are to Me, the more you will hate the things of this world." I could sense my standard of righteousness growing stronger and stronger.

AUTHENTIC WORSHIP

The next phrase to focus on in Romans 12:1 is "experiencing all that delights his heart." I used to read that and think, *Wow, God wants to give me the desires of my heart.* Don't get me wrong! This is true—God does want to give me the desires of my heart. But the more I meditated on this scripture, the more I saw that it's not about my desires that I think up on my own. It's about *His* desires.

Now, let's be honest. Your dreams and desires barely change your life. They aren't high enough. So how are they going to change the lives of those around you? Honestly, they can't! That's why you have to ask God to replace your desires with His desires. You need to ask Him to switch out your dreams for His. In this way, His dreams and plans for your life will not only change your life but also the lives of those around you.

The next phrase in this verse is powerful: "This becomes your genuine expression of worship." In other words, presenting yourself as a living sacrifice is what God wants you to do as an expression of your worship of Him. Being a living sacrifice should be your lifestyle.

I believe that fasting and praying is a lifestyle, not merely a one-time event. Because it pleases God for us to fast and pray, it should be something that we do on a regular basis. The length of the fast could be a single meal. What matters is that we choose to make God and His Word our focus above all else. That honors the Lord, and it will produce change in us every time.

In God's mind, the humble surrender of fasting and prayer is a genuine authentic expression of worship. God doesn't want something fake from you. No one likes a fake relationship, and God is no exception. He wants you to be authentic with Him.

> *Stop imitating the ideals and opinions of the culture around you, but be inwardly transformed by the Holy Spirit through a total reformation of how you think. This will empower you to discern God's will as you live a beautiful life, satisfying and perfect in his eyes.*
>
> Romans 12:2 TPT

I love this verse because it unravels the next beautiful truth about fasting in the very first phrase: "Stop imitating the ideals and opinions of the culture around you." We are to be imitators of God.

I remember the first time I fasted for 40 days. I had people lined up telling me I was crazy. I had doctors tell me that what I was doing was unhealthy. I had youth laughing at me because I wasn't eating. I had my own leaders laughing at me.

But the funny thing about it all was that I didn't care. All I cared about was what God thought about me. I didn't care about other people's opinions. In other words, I was set free from the fear of man. I could not have cared less. All I cared about was God's opinion.

I wasn't always that way. I used to care too much what people thought of me. But through fasting, the character of God was being developed in me. As His nature was revealed to me through His Word, I began to yield more and more to the Holy Spirit in prayer for God's own character traits to be developed in my life. I exercised my faith to grow in the grace of God. As a result, strong conviction grew in me.

Through fasting and prayer, you will develop a strong spirit that will not cave in to the fear of man. Man's opinion will not intimidate you. Man's money will not control you. You cannot be bought because with every decision you make to put His Word into your spirit instead of putting food into your mouth, you are growing strong through Jesus Christ.

The more you spend time with God in prayer, seeking Him, listening to Him, and aligning your thoughts with His, His opinion alone will become supreme in your life. A holy, reverential fear of the Lord will make His approval alone all that you care about and seek.

Romans 12 is so encouraging to me. If you grab hold of the words in verses 1 and 2, it will be life changing for you. The phrase that holds the key is this: "but be inwardly trans-formed." As you fast and pray, waiting upon the Lord and exchanging your thoughts and ways for His, the Holy Spirit will transform the way you think.

As your thoughts come more and more into agreement with God's will, your perspective changes. You will not only see Him as He is according to His Word, but you will also begin to see and identify yourself in agreement with how God sees you—as His beloved son or daughter. You will not think like a servant who believes he isn't worth anything and is unworthy to receive anything. Instead, your thoughts will be conformed to align with God's thoughts. You will draw your identity from Him and see yourself as a child of the King. You will acknowledge and accept your rights and authority in the Kingdom of Heaven from your Heavenly Father, who has much to impart to and bestow upon His children.

The best ideas, messages, and songs I have ever received from Heaven were the result of time spent in fasting and prayer.

While ministering to the Lord in fasting, giving myself to extended time in His Word and prayer instead of eating, I was increasingly aware of the Father's heart and His thoughts and desires. I could sense Him aligning me with His perfect plan as I yielded myself to His Spirit. I could distinguish more clearly His direction or revelation insights.

I have found that during times of fasting and ministering to the Lord, Romans 12:2 (TPT) becomes your reality: He will "empower you to discern God's will as you live a beautiful life, satisfying and perfect in his eyes."

There may be times when it seems as though you don't know what to do or where to turn. Remember, God gives grace to the humble (*see* 1 Pet. 5:5). By choosing to present yourself to the Lord in a posture of humility through fasting and prayer, the Holy Spirit will illuminate your understanding and realign your thoughts to be in sync with the perfect will of God.

When you come into agreement with God in that way, you will be filled with "knowing." His truth will flood you with light, enabling you to see His plan for you. And the grace of God will teach you what steps you need to take to see His will accomplished in your life (*see* Tit. 2:11-13).

So if you are walking in a place of darkness, in a place of not knowing what you need to know, just know that in His light, God will cause you to see light. He will reveal His plan to you through your time spent with Him in prayer and fasting.

MY PRAYER

Father, I thank You for teaching me how to imitate Your heart. I know that through my fasting and prayer, You are teaching me to be like You. I submit to You in everything I am. I understand that fasting and prayer positions me in a place of deep humility as I submit to You to strengthen and change me daily. I choose to crucify my flesh, and I commit to becoming a living sacrifice, holy and pleasing to You. I know that when I do this, I am aligning myself to Your perfect will. I understand that as I do this, I will not conform to the world but to Your way of doing things. I receive Your instruction in the name of Jesus. Amen.

CHAPTER 3

BIBLE HEROES WHO FASTED

THE OLD AND New Testaments give many examples of people who prayed and fasted in times of worship, consecration, or crisis. Aware of their total dependence upon God—whether outnumbered by enemies, threatened with death, or simply needing to know the wisdom of God—these men and women fasted and prayed.

Queen Esther, for example, when she was facing the genocide of all of the Jews living in Persia, called for the Jews to join her in three days of fasting without food or drink. Before she approached the most powerful king in the world regarding their deliverance and protection, Queen Esther clothed herself in humility before God.

These men and woman humbled themselves to silence their flesh and at times their own fears. They inclined their ears to hear God's voice. And in those moments, they received plans and blueprints, strategies to save nations, direction for ministry, and courage to fulfill destiny. Prayer and fasting helped them close out the clamor of the world. And in their stillness before God, they heard God's voice and kept their lives on track with His purpose and destiny for them.

The different types of fasts acknowledged in the Bible are:

1. Vegetables and fruits
2. Water and liquids only
3. No food or drink

All forms of fasting and prayer are a spiritual weapon. Let's take a look at a few who fasted in the Bible so we can learn principles not only from how and why they fasted, but also from what was accomplished during and after they fasted.

How Daniel Fasted

Let's take a look at the scripture that describes how Daniel fasted:

> *At that time I, Daniel, mourned for three weeks. I ate no choice food; no meat or wine touched my lips; and I used no lotions at all until the three weeks were over.*
>
> Daniel 10:2-3

This is a very interesting statement. Daniel said that he "mourned" for three weeks. This was an intensely focused time of concentration in prayer. Mourning and praying before the Lord indicates that Daniel was humbling his soul in prayer, making intercessions for his people. For three weeks, Daniel lay on his face before God to seek answers and intervention regarding the time of Israel's captivity in Babylon. Daniel mourned, fasted, and prayed earnestly.

The kind of prayer Daniel described as mourning was the Hebrew word *abal*, which means "to grieve." This kind of prayer reminds me of the intense prayer that preceded revivals that happened in the United States, ignited by the intercession of a man named Daniel Nash. If you want to know more about his life, please read the book *Daniel Nash: Prevailing Prince of Prayer* by J. Paul Reno.

Prayer and Fasting to Break Strongholds and Release Revival

Daniel Nash was a prayer warrior who would go into a city before the evangelist Charles Finney arrived to conduct meetings. Father Nash, as they called him, would rent a room where he would lay on the floor fasting, praying, and crying out to God to release revival in that city. Daniel Nash would agonize or "mourn" in travail and fasting until he knew that spiritual bondage was broken over that region. Then, when Finney arrived in the city to preach, souls would be swept into the Kingdom of God as the Holy Spirit was poured out because of that kind of prayer and fasting.

Finney was persuaded that it was the prayer and fasting of Daniel Nash that preceded the power, breaking strongholds and releasing revival. In fact, Finney so relied upon the prayer and fasting of Daniel Nash—which consistently resulted in a powerful work of the Holy Spirit to convict and thoroughly convert most of his audience—that within three or four months after Daniel Nash died, Finney left his itinerant ministry for the pastorate.

I believe that this was the kind of prayer that was offered up by Daniel, empowering angels—including Michael, one of the chief celestial princes—to push past spiritual opposition and to break through demonic strongholds.

WHY DANIEL FASTED

As Daniel sought the Lord through prayer and fasting regarding the fate of Israel after the 70 years of Babylonian captivity, the spiritual world was unveiled before him in a vision. He saw the angel Michael, who called him highly esteemed and let him know that he was heard from the very first day he began to pray. The angelic messenger was dispatched to bring Daniel the answer to his prayer.

Daniel was well known in Heaven's courts because of his fasting and fervent prayers. In fact, we find two powerful principles that Daniel activated as he sought the Lord in fasting:

1. Daniel set his mind to gain understanding.

2. Daniel set his mind to humble himself.

Through fasting, we set our mind to seek the Lord, His wisdom, strength, and understanding. We see in other passages that when confronted with difficulty or danger, Daniel set himself to inquire of the Lord and gain understanding (*see* Dan. 2:17-22). The end result each time was a response from Heaven to Daniel's inquiry.

Fasting is a deliberate choice to humble yourself. As a result, God answers because He draws near to give grace to the humble. When you deliberately set your mind to come into agreement with God, praying out His words by the direction of His Spirit, angels hearken to the voice of His words through you. And when angels start to work on your behalf, they will fight and oppose the demonic forces that would try to hinder and oppose you in your call.

The angel told Daniel that his prayers were heard from the first day, yet it took the angel another 20 days to bring Daniel the answer he was waiting for. Why? Verse 13 tells us: The prince of Persia resisted the angel. In other words, the angel was in spiritual warfare for 21 days with that demonic principality ruling over Persia.

This shows us that demonic forces are designated over countries and regions. They are persistent in their warfare, but their evil influence can be broken through fasting and praying.

The devil did not want Daniel to receive his answer from Heaven, but Daniel's prayer broke through all opposition against him. Daniel prevailed in prayer to receive the wisdom and understanding necessary for him to complete his call as he interceded for the freedom of his nation.

God is no respecter of persons. The same applies to you and me. He will respond to our prayers and grant us understanding when we set ourselves to seek His will in humility.

SPIRITUAL LESSONS OF THE DANIEL FAST

1. The spiritual world was unveiled.

2. Daniel's name was well known and highly esteemed in Heaven.

3. Daniel's fasted lifestyle maintained a constant posture of spiritual humility.

4. Daniel's prayer was heard from day one.

5. Daniel's prayer caused angels to work on his behalf.

6. Daniel's prayer caused angels to fight on his behalf.

7. Daniel's fast caused a demonic force over a nation to be broken.

As you fast and pray, you can expect results just as Daniel experienced. You may not have an open vision or see an angel, but you will hear from Heaven and you will receive divine assistance!

Fasting doesn't change God, but it puts you in position to work with God. Angels will hearken to the voice of His words coming through your mouth when you pray and decree. And when you obey God and yield to Him in humility, He will release grace and favor to you that will open doors that no man can open and that no man can shut.

When you enter into a Daniel fast with the same motivation Daniel had—to set your mind to humble yourself and to understand—you will find that this powerful tool will bring you powerful results. All of this is available to you and me. All you have to do is hear and obey when God prompts you to start fasting.

Do not start without being prompted by the Holy Spirit's direction. Fasting done in the flesh is pointless and torture! Fasting done in the Spirit is a supernatural weapon.

To ignore this weapon would be foolish because it has been given to us to dismantle the enemy and overcome all of his tactics. Through fasting and prayer, we align ourselves on the Lord's side, and He fights our battles for us.

ALL LIQUIDS: THE NEHEMIAH FAST

Nehemiah served as the cupbearer to Artaxerxes, the emperor of Persia and the son of King Xerxes, whom we find in the book of Esther. As the cupbearer to the king, Nehemiah's responsibility was to take a test sip of the wine, juice, or water that was given to the king. This was necessary because a common way of assassination was to poison the king's drink. This would mean that Nehemiah was risking his life every single day for the well-being of the Persian emperor.

In examining aspects of Nehemiah's life and responsibilities, we see that his character traits reflected a lifestyle of humility, self-discipline, and integrity. These qualities were strengthened and fine-tuned by his continual devotion to the Lord, which certainly included times of deliberate and focused fasting and prayer.

During this time of serving King Artaxerxes, Nehemiah received word about the exiles who were back in Jerusalem. They were unprotected because there was no wall around the city. He was in distress, and it says that he fasted for certain days.

And it came to pass, when I heard these words,
that I sat down and wept, and mourned certain

days, and fasted, and prayed before the God of heaven.

Nehemiah 1:4 KJV

The Bible doesn't specify how many days Nehemiah fasted, so that leads me to believe that it was more than three days. Another thing the Bible doesn't specify is the type of fast this was. Normally the Bible says exactly what kind of fast someone was engaged in. The logical suggestion is that this was a liquid fast. Whatever kind of fast it was, it brought great results.

My personal experience in a liquid fast is to drink mainly water and juices. Of course, in our day and age, we could add tea or coffee, but it can cause you to feel horrible if you're not drinking enough water. It is important to note that the liquid that gives you the most strength is water. And not all water is the same. Most don't realize that normal bottled water is acidic. Therefore, it is more beneficial to your body if you can find water with a pH balance above 7.5, or alkaline water. That is a personal preference, but it may prove helpful to you as well.

In a liquid fast, depending on what the Lord has told you to do, you can have water, juices, vegetable broth, tea, or coffee. It's really up to you and the Lord. Water will always bring refreshment, whereas juice is acidic and will trigger hunger. Coffee with caffeine can dehydrate you. Too much juice might cause your stomach to hurt. I've been there and done that.

Remember, this is not a diet! True Bible fasting is not a diet or a way to lose weight, but a benefit of fasting is that you can lose weight and rest your body by detoxifying it into wholeness.

Fasting is a dedicated act of worship, where your main source of energy is derived from your time spent with the Lord. The correct way to fast is to devote the time to the Lord that you would normally spend eating. This devotion is described in Job 23:12 (NKJV): "I have treasured the words of His mouth more than my necessary food."

Devoting increased time and attention to God's Word and His presence is the only way fasting will give you the strength to pursue and align yourself to the will of God for your life. That focused pursuit is an expression of faith that pleases God—faith that will surely see His plans come to pass.

BENEFITS OF NEHEMIAH'S FASTING AND PRAYING

Nehemiah's private posture of heart before the Lord in prayer and fasting produced a public release of divine favor and strength to equip him for the task of rebuilding the wall of Jerusalem. As Nehemiah humbled himself through fasting:

1. God caused the world to help Nehemiah in his assignment.

2. God caused courage to arise within him.

3. Nehemiah birthed the plan and the strategy to fulfill his assignment.

4. The hand of God came upon Nehemiah.

5. God established Nehemiah's authority publicly, dealing with the opposition against him.

Nehemiah faced great opposition as he worked on the wall, but through fasting and prayer that opposition was taken care of ahead of time.

I recall one year when I fasted constantly. I would finish one fast, and God would put me on another. I would wake up the next morning excited to eat, and God would say it's time to fast.

Finally, after almost a year of this, I asked the Lord: "Why are You asking me to fast so much?"

I sensed the Lord's reply: "Philip, your fasting invited Me to defeat opposition and to remove obstacles before you get to them. There are many things that will try to oppose you, but they won't be able to do it because you have already taken care of them in prayer."

Fasting is a weapon that defeats the enemy at faraway distances. In Ephesians 6, we read about the whole armor of God. It's a powerful chapter about our authority in Christ. All the weapons of a Roman soldier are listed except one—the javelin! A skilled Roman soldier would throw that spear great distances to defeat the enemy before he got there. Some theologians believe the javelin is the weapon of prayer and supplication. It's not called the spear of prayer, but it is listed in the list of weapons in our spiritual armory. (You can read more about this and about the full armor of God in the book my dad, Rick Renner, wrote entitled *Dressed to Kill*.)

Nehemiah understood this principle, and through prayer and fasting he paved the way for the wall to be built. Then 52 days later, Nehemiah accomplished the dream God placed in his heart.

God wants to fulfill the dreams that are in your heart. Fasting and praying will strengthen you spiritually to defeat obstacles the enemy tries to put in your path. Not only that, but fasting and prayer will also pave the way for you to accomplish what God has put on your heart.

JESUS

Before Jesus even started His fast, He was baptized by John the Baptist, and God's audible voice came from Heaven, saying, "This is My beloved Son, in whom I am well pleased" (Matt. 3:17 NKJV). I recall one morning when Pastor Paul Brady, the pastor I served with at Millennial Church in Tulsa, Oklahoma, was preaching on this subject, and he brought up a point that I thought was amazing and thought-provoking.

Pastor Paul said, "As Christians, the immediate thing that we expect when we are called out in a meeting and given a prophetic word is *Finally! Breakthrough is happening.* I have been praying, faithfully crying out. I have received the prophetic word, and now everything is going to get better. My problems will be gone. But that didn't happen to Jesus! After He heard the audible voice of God, He was sent to the desert! Yet as Christians, we often expect immediate breakthrough without a desert."

This tells me that there are two possible reactions to a prophetic word, which is meant to encourage and to equip:

1. I can relax and do nothing because the breakthrough is here.

2. I can recognize that God is challenging me to go higher, which means more sacrifice and growth on my part!

It could mean that the blessing is coming, but there will be a fight, with possibly a desert experience in front of you. This is not a popular message to preach in the church, yet this was the reality that Jesus faced after He heard the audible voice of the Father.

It's encouraging to know that when we receive a revelation from God's Word or a prophetic word, this could mean our victory is close. However, it could also mean that pressure is about to grow because responsibility will grow. And, of course, that means opposition to your assignment will grow.

The truth is, that word God speaks to you will prepare you for the future. In my personal life, every strategic word from God that I have received has meant more responsibility; yet it has also strengthened and equipped me for the future. This is what happened with Jesus.

In the desert, Jesus was tested. The Bible does not say Jesus was thirsty, but it does say He was hungry. Therefore, we understand He went without food. Extreme temperatures in the wilderness would be strenuous to live in without shelter. Jesus' strength would have been received when He was baptized, and it was secured by His consistent communion with the Heavenly Father. In other words, Jesus' source of life and strength during those 40 days in the wilderness would have been the presence of God—and that's it.

The Bible tells us in Matthew 4:1-2:

> *Then Jesus was led by the Spirit into the wilderness to be tempted by the devil. After fasting forty days and forty nights, he was hungry.*

This is such an interesting passage of Scripture. Satan tempted Jesus in three different ways in the wilderness—and these are the same ways he will tempt you and me today. I think it's important to take note that during fasts directed of the Lord, these same temptations will come to test you as well.

1. The devil will tempt you to misuse your ability according to his instructions, trying to provoke you to follow his orders and not the leading of the Spirit. For example: "Turn these stones into bread to satisfy your hunger" (*see* Matt. 4:3).

2. Satan will challenge your identity and your understanding of your covenant privileges as a son or daughter of God. For example: "If you are a Son, take this risk and see if your Father's angels will rescue you" (*see* Matt. 4:6).

3. The devil offered Jesus the world—a fast track to influence—in exchange for His worship

because the object of His worship and desire would control Him (*see* Matt. 4:8). In this temptation, Satan attacked Jesus' authority, humility, destiny, and self-worth.

JESUS CHOSE THE PATH THAT LED TO OUR VICTORY IN HIM

I want to concentrate a little more on this last point. Many times in our Christian walk, we are offered the same path by the devil. The truth is, that path is evil, but let's remember that he masquerades as an angel of light (*see* 2 Cor. 11:14). That being said, if we fall into that trap, it will become the cage that never allows us to reach our full potential—or you could say it will clip our wings, resulting in our never soaring as eagles.

Often, the devil will dangle opportunities in front of our eyes. In this way, he is challenging our pride. It might be that the route he is dangling in front of us is the easy route without challenges but immediate results. Maybe that route will seem financially stronger, more comfortable, and filled with the approval of man. But if it is not God's will, it will ultimately cause you to lose your call.

This is the part in the road where many believers take a wrong turn and lose it all, deceived into thinking they have chosen the better part.

Each one of us will face this test. What route will we choose? Will we choose immediate satisfaction or the chiseling of our character as we learn to trust and rely fully on God?

Will we choose the highway of pride or the pathway of humility? Jesus chose humility. He chose the Cross.

In this last temptation, Satan tried to make Jesus a partaker of his own nature—pride. The first Adam bowed his knee in obedience to Satan's words and embraced Satan's fallen nature for all mankind. But Jesus, the last Adam, stood on the authority of God's Word and declared His allegiance to God alone. In that moment, Jesus settled it. The strength of God was made perfect in His weakness. At the end of His fast, Jesus conquered His own flesh; He resisted the devil; and He walked out of the wilderness in the power of the Spirit.

Having presented every scheme and angle, the devil failed. He was defeated, and Jesus was victorious.

Jesus was challenged in His:

- Identity
- Physical weakness
- Obedience to the Word
- Humility
- Devotion and love for His Father

In every area, Jesus stood triumphant. And in His prayer and fasting, He paved the way for us to follow Him in that same victory.

In a fast, in your calling, and throughout your life, Satan will challenge you in these same areas. He does not know any new tricks. He has done the same thing over and over for thousands of years to billions of people. This makes him predictable, and if you are led by the Spirit as Jesus was, you will be able to catch and conquer the enemy at his own game.

Jesus answered Satan with the Word of God. The Word was strengthened within Jesus as He fasted and prayed. The same applies to you and me. After we have fasted and prayed—whether it was for one meal or for one month, God's strength will be made perfect in us to oppose what comes to oppose us. So when Satan comes to tempt, challenge, and question us, just like Jesus, you and I will maintain our devotion to the Father, answer him with the Word, and move forward in the power of the Spirit—victorious every time.

FASTING UNLOCKS WISDOM, DIVINE STRATEGIES, AND DIRECTION

Moses

Moses twice went for 40 days without food or water. That is actually physically impossible, but Moses was sustained by the literal manifest presence of God. Fully consumed by God in the realm of God, His natural physical need for food was supernaturally suspended. There, in the Spirit, Moses received the Ten Commandments, which are the standard for Judeo-Christian morality to this day. He also received a blueprint with exact, strict instructions to the tiniest detail on how to build according to that model (*see* Heb. 8:5).

Joshua

We can say without a doubt that Moses received supernatural strength and revelation as he met with God on the holy mountain. But all that time, Joshua was on the side of the mountain, waiting for Moses. I believe Joshua was also fasting along with his leader.

This is a beautiful picture of discipleship. Moses was on the mountain receiving a direct download from God while his disciple Joshua had joined hands with him in the Spirit to pray for him during that same duration of time.

Elijah

After Elijah beheaded the prophets of Baal and literally called fire down from Heaven, Jezebel threatened to kill him, so Elijah fled. When he finally stopped running, an angel came and fed him. Elijah took a nap, and when he woke up the angel fed him again. Then it says that Elijah traveled for 40 days. The angel's food sustained Elijah for 40 days until he reached Mount Horeb, the same mountain where Moses received the Ten Commandments (known to us as Mount Sinai; see 1 Kings 19:4-8).

On the mountain, God revealed Himself to Elijah.

> *The Lord said, "Go out and stand on the mountain in the presence of the Lord, for the Lord is about to pass by." Then a great and powerful wind tore the mountains apart and shattered the rocks before the Lord, but the Lord was not in the wind. After the wind there was an earthquake, but the Lord was not in the earthquake. After the earthquake came a fire, but the Lord was not in the fire. And after the fire came a gentle whisper. When Elijah heard it, he pulled his cloak over his face and went out and stood at the mouth of the cave. Then a voice said to him, "What are you doing here, Elijah?"*
>
> 1 Kings 19:11-13

This passage of Scripture is one of my favorites. It shows an extremely valuable principle that is strengthened through fasting and prayer: *The volume of the noise and business of life turns down and becomes much quieter when you are fasting and praying.*

Let's consider what took place in this passage:

First, Elijah felt and heard a powerful wind that tore apart the mountains and that shattered the rock, but the Lord was not in the wind.

Next, an earthquake took place on the mountain.

Right after that, fire came, but the Lord was not in any of it.

Finally, Elijah heard a gentle whisper, and God was in a whisper. Let that sink in again: God was in a whisper.

If you really want to hear God, you will have to turn off every distraction. Sometimes life becomes way too noisy. Life is so busy that we can become too busy to listen to the Lord's gentle whisper. If you don't want to listen to God, He will not shout at you. God will gently whisper, and if you are not attentive to His still, small voice, you will miss what He has to say to you.

FASTING HELPS YOU HEAR THE VOICE OF GOD MORE CLEARLY

I remember the time I was invited to my first big youth conference. I was preparing to preach, and I heard God say, "Fall on your face before Me." This was during worship, but it was not during a slow song when it would be appropriate to fall on my face before God. It was during a fast-paced song. Everyone was jumping and excited, so it made no sense for me to lay down on my face before God. Plus, the floor was dirty. I had every excuse to not fall on my knees, and all my excuses made sense.

First of all, no one ever falls on his face during a fast song. That is not appropriate! Second, I was about to preach and lying on my face would mean my jeans and shirt would get dirty, making me look terrible on stage. Still, I recognized His voice. I knew what I had to do. I fell down on one knee first. Then I heard the Lord say, "That's not what I asked you to do! I said fall on your face!"

I went to two knees, believing that I could go halfway in my obedience, and it would be okay. But God said, "No—on your face."

Finally, I lay on my face and just began to worship Him. My flesh was screaming; my mind was racing with all my excuses. But after I began to worship, the voice of my flesh became quieter and quieter. Finally, I could hear His voice.

I heard it again: "On your face!"

This time I lay completely on the floor with my forehead resting on my hands. I just couldn't get up. I tried, but His presence was so strong! I heard, "I'm not finished with you yet."

Then it happened—He started revealing all of His plans for my life.

To this day, that is one the most memorable and precious times that I have had with the Lord. The amazing thing is that I almost missed it. If I would not have listened to that still small voice, I would have missed God speaking into my life in a profound way.

In all of this, God was teaching me not to fear man's opinion. I could feel man's opinion all around me. I could feel what seemed to be like 50 people looking down at me, thinking, *What is he doing on his face during a fast song? There's something just not right about that!* God was teaching me that the only opinion that truly matters is His opinion.

That's what happens in a fast. You begin to value only God's opinion, and you really could not care less about what other people say. There is a supernatural power that comes on you! In that place of fellowship with the Father, you don't fear or overestimate everyone else's opinion.

But I didn't get there immediately. My flesh was desperately trying to get out of what the Lord was telling me to do. But God had different plans for me. I had so many reasons why I should not fall on my face, but God was teaching me a lesson that I would remember for the rest of my life.

Fasting and praying will cause you to hear that still small voice loud and clear, just like Elijah did. All the other distractions of life fade into the background while God's voice becomes the main focus. And when God speaks, nothing else matters.

My Prayer

Father, I thank You for teaching me the benefits of praying and fasting. I receive the wisdom of these principles, and I understand that as I fast and pray, the unseen is becoming seen because of the grace of God that has been lavished upon me. The enemy has been stripped of all authority.

Therefore, I know that the victory is mine, and I take it!

Thank You for revealing both spiritual and practical principles as I fast. Just as Daniel and Nehemiah understood that fasting paved the way before them, I will also walk in that same understanding and authority. I will not ignore this powerful weapon You have given me, but I will use it to build the Kingdom. Just as Jesus yielded Himself to You without restraint through fasting and prayer, I will do the same. Because I choose to hide Your Word in my heart that I may not sin against You, Your Word will rise up and speak through me when I am challenged, questioned, and tempted to take the easy route instead of trusting in You.

I understand, as Elijah did, that Your voice is not in the busyness of life but in the still small voice, so I will focus all my attention on following that voice in my spirit. Holy Spirit, teach me every day to follow hard after the Father's heart. I give You my all. In the name of Jesus, I pray. Amen.

CHAPTER 4

A New Wineskin:
What Jesus Said
About Fasting and Prayer

I THINK IT is powerful that when Jesus preached about fasting, He had great experience in that area. Jesus began His ministry with a 40-day fast in the wilderness, and when He was at His weakest point physically after eating no food and drinking only water, it was then that He defeated the devil with the Word of God that sustained Him.

Jesus didn't just "talk the talk"; He "walked the walk." He gave Himself continually to prayer, often rising a great while before daylight to meet with the Father. Therefore, Jesus' consecration authorized and gave Him jurisdiction to speak on the subject of fasting with great authority. But beyond the truth of Jesus' authorization to speak about fasting was the manifestation of power He demonstrated as a direct result of His lifestyle of prayer and fasting.

We read several times in the gospels where Jesus talked about the motive and the purpose of our fasting. But Jesus never said whether we should or should not fast. He simply said, "When you fast."

This lets us know that it was understood that fasting is to have a role in our lives. Fasting was not only important under the Old Covenant, but Jesus also confirmed it would remain important under the New Covenant as well.

We know this is true because when the disciples of John approached Jesus to ask Him why His disciples didn't fast like they did, Jesus replied, "The days will come when the bridegroom will be taken away from them; then they will fast" (Luke 5:35 NKJV). This statement then led into the most profound truth as Jesus expressed the purpose or the result of fasting—a truth revealed in the meaning of "the new wineskin."

But first, let's consider what Jesus said about how to enter into a fast.

> *When you fast, do not look somber as the hypocrites do, for they disfigure their faces to show others they are fasting. Truly I tell you, they have received their reward in full. But when you fast, put oil on your head and wash your face, so that it will not be obvious to others that you are fasting, but only to your Father, who is unseen; and your Father, who sees what is done in secret will reward you.*
>
> Matthew 6:16-18

In this passage, Jesus is clear that our heart posture in a fast is to be one of humility and not pride. We don't fast to be seen of men but to humble ourselves before God. God resists the proud, but He gives grace to the humble (*see* James 4:6).

While fasting, we are often presented with opportunities to be the hypocrite Jesus warned us about. Of course, none of us want to believe we could ever slip into prideful, self-righteous behavior, but our flesh is quick to seek every opportunity to express itself in that way. This is one of the main reasons to make fasting a part of our lifestyle—to silence the voice and tendencies of the flesh.

THE PATH OF PRIDE OR HUMILITY?

Allow me to present two scenarios taken from the pages of a chapter of immaturity in my own life while I was fasting. Thankfully, the Lord helped me realize that I had displeased Him and how I had done it. I repented of such behavior and asked God to forgive me.

Many times when you fast, you have the opportunity to let people know you're fasting. Have you ever noticed that, when you commit to a fast, someone always seems to invite you out to eat?

It's a challenge to pass that test while aromas of savory dishes fill the air—especially when your friend says, "Order whatever you like; I'm paying." In that moment, you have two choices. You can say, "I'll just have water because I'm fasting," or you can say, "I'll just have water because I'm not eating right now."

Honestly, in that moment your flesh will scream its thoughts to your mind, *Tell him that you're fasting! He will think that you are spiritual and then he will respect you even more.*

But then you will hear reason come into play, saying, "Well, you can't lie to him, so tell him the truth! You can't say you are not hungry, because that is lying. You are starving, so you have to tell him the truth!"

In this simple scenario, what do you do? You follow what your spirit is saying: Remember Jesus' words. You don't show you are tired; you don't show that you are hungry; you don't show any pain; and you don't disfigure your face. Instead, you speak to yourself to put on the strength of Christ like a garment, smile, and ignore the hunger pain in your stomach.

It is very clear in the Scriptures that you are not to make it obvious that you are fasting. The correct answer is, "I'll just have water."

Of course, the friend's immediate response is "Why?" Honestly, your flesh wants him to ask that question so that you can brag to him that you are fasting and that this is your tenth day! This is what your flesh is screaming about, but Jesus said not to make it obvious that you are fasting.

What that means for me is to do everything in my power not to tell people I am fasting. If they eventually figure it out, I do not have to tell them how long the fast is going to last.

Another scenario of what Jesus tells you not to do might occur when a friend invites you to eat. You reply: "I'm not eating." Your friend may simply reply, "Okay," and let it drop. But then you try to figure a way to put fasting into the conversation. I know because I have done it!

This, of course, is awkward because now your friend realizes that you just want to talk about fasting because you are on a fast. Then the conversation becomes all about you instead of what God intended for you to talk about.

You may feel so spiritual, but there is a flip side to the whole situation. Some people may think that you are a spiritual believer and be impressed—but mature believers will recognize you are full of pride.

I have ignorantly put myself in that situation and then left the conversation realizing my words only glorified self, not Christ. I repented and asked God's forgiveness, but the damage had already been done. Usually, people will not call you back when they think you spoke pridefully and in arrogance.

Jesus said hypocrites want their actions on full display as they boastfully walk the road of prideful self-exaltation. There is another path, however, that is unseen. That is the path of humility. On that path, no one sees your fast because you do not blab about it. And where there is humility, wisdom will follow (*see* Prov. 11:2). When God sees your humility before Him in private, He will reward you openly before men in due time.

As we submit to God through fasting, pride is revealed and replaced with humility. Living a fasted lifestyle keeps us in a place of continual surrender, walking the path of humility, which will be evident in every area of our lives—starting with the way we do or do not speak.

Humility will cause you to keep your mouth shut. Proverbs is extremely clear on this:

*Do not boast about tomorrow, for you do not
know what a day may bring. Let someone else
praise you, and not your own mouth; an outsider,
and not your own lips.*

Proverbs 27:1-2

Scripture is clear that you shouldn't boast about yourself. There have been times when the Lord has told me to shut my mouth and stop talking. At that moment, everything in me wanted to talk about my accomplishments and what I had done so that people would think well about me. When I listened to His still, small voice and remained silent, the very thing that I needed to have said about me came through another person's mouth.

Through experiences like that, the Lord showed me that I don't have to promote myself; He will do it when and how He desires. In those times, I'm so happy God told me to shut my mouth.

When you allow God to set you forward instead of trying to do it yourself, it's always better His way. Through fasting, God will teach you to shut your mouth, both physically and spiritually. As you allow a spirit of humility to control your mouth, your conversation will produce godly communication, and you will find that God is also chiseling your character to produce wisdom.

*When swelling and pride come, then emptiness
and shame come also, but with the humble (those
who are lowly, who have been pruned or chiseled*

> *by trial, and renounce self) are skillful and godly*
> *Wisdom and soundness.*
>
> Proverbs 11:2 AMPC

Godly character is revealed through right words. But it is formed by right choices, such as the willingness to sacrifice the immediate gratification of food for a desired goal or breakthrough.

WHEN YOU FAST, YOUR FAMILY ALSO SACRIFICES

There are some situations where you cannot hide your fast, and I would even say it's wrong to do so. Before I go on a fast, I make sure I am in unity with my wife. Ella has always been a great pillar of strength for me through all of the fasts I have ever gone through. I cannot and will not hide it from her. I need her strength to accomplish what God has called me to do.

It would be selfish for me to say that I am the only one who sacrifices during a fast, because it is a sacrifice for the whole family. Think about it—sharing a meal is a form of fellowship for a family. So if you are not eating, there is a sacrifice of fellowship taking place.

Usually, a family gets home in the evening and eats together. For me, in times of fasting, I sit at the table with my family to fellowship, but I do not eat. We have all been in the situations when one person eats at the table and the other says, "I will just have some water." It can feel awkward for everyone. Family is no exception.

After I am finished drinking my water, I need strength, so I go to my room, shut the door, and go to the Source of my strength, which is my daily relationship with God. Right before I shut the door, my kids might say, "Daddy, can you play with us?"

I reply, "Daddy needs to pray." Because I need strength!

My youngest daughter asks, "Why, Daddy?" I give the same answer.

Sometimes that discomfort causes tension, stress, and tears. The kids in turn ask Momma, "Is Daddy okay? What's wrong?"

Mom replies, "Daddy just needs some rest and needs to pray. He will be fine. When he gets done with the fast, he will be able to play, run, and pick you up on his shoulders again."

Then in the cutest way possible, I've had my youngest daughter pick up a cookie and try to give it to me because I needed strength. But I had to reply, "I am fasting right now. Daddy can't eat that cookie, but thank you. I love you, sweetie!"

You can't hide your hunger pain or fatigue from the family.

This kind of fatigue is only the case for fasts that are 40 days in length, and it usually happens toward the end. On fasts that are less than 40 days, I continue to play and wrestle with my kids.

Even in a fast, we still work and have responsibilities. Fasting does not give us an excuse to disengage and ignore all duties in the home.

My point in writing this is to explain that fasting with prayer doesn't just affect the person who is fasting—it affects the whole family.

I honor and thank my family for every time they have supported me. They see right past the smile I keep on my face, no matter how I feel. They ask, "How are you really doing?"

At that point, I say, "I'm tired, and I'd really like a hug. And I need to pray!"

You set off for bed, still in pain or feeling fatigue. Your wife realizes it's probably not a good time to talk. Before she even begins a conversation, you are already snoring. Before she goes to bed, she is praying for you, and through it all, she puts her trust in God, believing that the fast is changing things in the Spirit and the unseen will soon become seen.

Because your body is not processing food, you do not need an alarm clock. You wake very early the next morning, not needing a lot of sleep. Then the day starts all over again with prayer and the source of your strength found in your relationship with God.

I could continue to write about different scenarios I have experienced that can happen in the family during a fast, but I believe my point has been made. A fast is a sacrifice, not just for the person who is fasting but for the whole family.

It would be an exaggeration for me to say that the types of scenarios I described above happen every day. They are scenarios that happen on the days you are losing weight. Your body feels it, so the family feels it. And as a result, the whole family needs to press into God.

That's why I greatly honor my family in supporting me through the years, especially my wife. Ella steadfastly encourages me: "You can make it, Philip! God is with you!"

This scenario I have written happens several times in a long period of fasting. There are days when you must break through, but there are more days of happiness and joy.

Some days are easy. You sense a supernatural impartation of strength, creativity, and energy flowing. You're nearly vibrating under the power of God's grace upon you.

Just like there is a grace to fulfill different calls on every believer's life, there is a grace for fasting and praying—not only for the person fasting, but also for the entire family. But then there are days when the person fasting has to press in and focus to break through.

I have experienced all of it, and I have never regretted any of it. Without faith, which requires sacrifice, it is impossible to please God. But God is a rewarder of those who diligently seek Him (*see* Heb. 6:12). God honors the person who fasts and the family that honors God while that person fasts.

WHEN YOU FAST...

I was asked at a workshop, "If you're in an extended fast, do you still have intimacy with your wife?" The Bible addresses that specifically:

> *Abstaining from sex is permissible for a period of time if you both agree to it, and if it's for the purposes of prayer and fasting—but only for such times. Then come back together again. Satan has an ingenious way of tempting us when we least expect it.*
>
> 1 Corinthians 7:5 MSG

The key is agree to it. Be in agreement. If you have strength and there is unity, enjoy. But if you have no strength, rest! God will bless you in any case!

Also, use wisdom to communicate with those you might work with closely who are involved in your life, work, and ministry. Be certain to give understanding if you have limitations during this time so as not to cause friction and strife.

WHEN YOU PRAY...

When we minister to the Lord through prayer and fasting, it is a truly personal expression of worship. And the more we yield, the deeper our surrender becomes to intimacy in worship of the Father.

Humility is the key to sincere expressions of worship and love, and humility is at the core of effective prayer and fasting. Without humility, our prayers aren't heard and our fasting is pointless.

Jesus was clear about how we are to approach the Father in prayer: "Don't be like the hypocrites!" Hypocrites are all show. They care more about how they appear before men than they care about the attitude and condition of their heart before God. That's why Jesus always had a stern tone and rebuke for the hypocrites. They completely missed the point about what really mattered in order to please God.

Jesus even described how we should go before the Father in times of private prayer:

> *When you pray, don't be like the hypocrites who love to pray publicly on street corners and in the*

synagogues where everyone can see them. I tell you the truth, that is all the reward they will ever get. But when you pray, go away by yourself, shut the door behind you, and pray to your Father in private. Then your Father, who sees everything, will reward you.

Matthew 6:5-6 NLT

In this passage of Scripture, Jesus describes the approach we should take in intimate prayer with the Father. It's an attitude of humility in the posture of intimacy, taken to a place of privacy. *This kind of prayer will propel you into your future.*

Hypocrites pray in public so that everyone can see them, but the prayer of true intimacy and communion that God values, no one sees. Prayer behind a shut door with just you and God is the kind of prayer that truly sustains you in your walk with the Lord. This is true regardless of whether you are fasting or not.

This is the prayer expressed in a fasted lifestyle of reverence and surrender. This is the kind of prayer that prompted Jesus to rise a great while before daylight and go to private places to be alone with the Father (*see* Mark 1:35).

True growth in fasting and praying happens when you spend time with the Lord one on one with the door closed.

Relationships fail when there is no one-on-one time or intimacy. The same is true with your relationship with God. You have to have one-on-one time with the Lord to experience the ongoing awareness of His presence and to walk in the power of His Spirit.

You may think that you will survive on just church services, special meetings, and conferences—but you won't. Corporate gatherings are important, and they serve a purpose to strengthen our union with the Body, as well as to fortify our own function in it. But intimacy and personal communion with God in the secret place is a private fellowship that we must cultivate alone and one on one with the Father, just as Jesus did during His earthly ministry.

It is in the secret place that God will open up to you like never before.

> *I will give you hidden treasures, riches stored in secret places, so that you may know that I am the Lord, the God of Israel, who summons you by name.*
>
> Isaiah 45:3

The strongest times that I have ever had with the Lord in prayer have been when no one was around. No music. No church service. No schedule. Just me and Jesus spending time with each other in the early hours of the morning. It has been in those times that I have received messages, songs, and direction that challenged me and compelled me to grow in my walk with God. It has been in those times that the unsearchable things I do not know become known to me, revealed to my heart by the Spirit of God.

> *Call to me and I will answer you and tell you great and unsearchable things you do not know.*
>
> Jeremiah 33:3

In the secret place, the hidden things become revealed. When you call unto God, He answers and shows you the riches stored away for you to access. Lack of understanding turns into direction, and weakness turns into strength— *there in the secret place!*

Many times, especially during fasting, your only source of energy is prayer.

There have been times when I felt tired, sick, and hungry, but after I spent a couple of hours with God, I felt fully energized and enthusiastic and endued with God's power. The Greek verb *enduo* means literally "to sink into." It also means to enter into, to get into, or to put on. That is what I experienced—the putting on of God's mighty power and strength.

But we have to participate in the putting on, just as we have to deliberately take off something else. An example of how we apply this word is found in Romans:

> *The night is far spent, the day is at hand: let us therefore cast off the works of darkness, and let us put on the armour of light.*
> Romans 13:12 KJV

When you go into that secret place, you take off anxiety and weakness and you put on the armor of light through prayer.

Any soldier in battle must take off his civilian clothes to put on armor. The same is true in prayer. We take off our pride and weakness, and we put on God's humility and strength. This is a process that should happen daily in our walk with the Lord, regardless of whether or not we are fasting.

Enduo should be a daily standard of our lives. We take off our dreams and put on God's dreams. We take off our ways and put on God's ways as we daily renew our minds with the mind of Christ through prayer and His Word.

You must remember that fasting and praying is warfare. As you fast and pray, your submission to God is in direct resistance of the enemy and strongholds that he has tried to put on you, your city, your country, and your assignment. Just like Daniel's fast was a war of aggressive resistance against demonic powers over the province of Western Asia, our reliance upon God as we fast is doing the same thing in resistance to break down strongholds.

> *The weapons we fight with are not the weapons of the world. On the contrary, they have divine power to demolish strongholds.*
>
> 2 Corinthians 10:4

SUPERNATURAL STRENGTH!

Just as fasting is a supernatural weapon against the enemy, it is a supernatural vehicle to transport you into the presence of God, where you connect with the Source of your strength. This has been true for me many times. One situation stands out to me in particular.

I was in Belarus, where I had just led worship for two hours. I was physically exhausted. It was the 36th day on an all-water fast. During this entire time, I drank water only two ways—cold or at room temperature. Honestly, I was to the point that I could barely stand the sight of water.

It was the sixth day of a ten-day tour. I felt like I was completely done. We had conducted a night of worship every day in different cities that were usually about 200 miles apart.

With all the constant travel, fasting, and nights of worship, I was weary and drained of physical strength.

My strength was gone. I knew the only way I was going to make it through the next four days and finish the fast and the tour would be through supernatural assistance. After singing on that 36th day of the fast, I had no more strength. (Note: Never do this kind of fast unless the Lord leads you to it. I had worked years to prepare myself spiritually and physically to do this kind of fast.)

I went to the green room, which was filled with equipment and bags from the tour team. As I sat in a little green chair, I told the Lord, "I can't do it anymore!"

Then I heard the Lord speak to me: "Philip, don't even pray. Your life has turned into a living prayer. Just rest in My presence."

One of my favorite scriptures in the Bible is Exodus 33:14: Your presence will go with me, and You will give me rest. I was in a place where I knew I needed *enduo*. I needed to take off my own striving and put on God's armor of rest.

As I sat in the chair and just surrendered everything I was to God, I felt what seemed like an IV go up my arm. Within seconds, I felt strength and energy that I knew was supernatural. It was as though I had just been fed angels' food.

To this day, I don't know exactly what took place in that supernatural transaction. All I know is that when I stripped off my striving and put on God's strength and rest, within seconds I felt like I had eaten and drunk the most amazing energy drink. I felt like pure adrenaline had been pumped into my body.

I picked up my bag that weighed 70 pounds, and I started carrying sound equipment and putting it into the van. That moment of *enduo* was enough for me to finish the tour and complete my 40-day fast.

During this fast, I saw miracles take place in every city where we ministered. There were miracles of healing and deliverances, and many people gave their lives to the Lord. I knew that I was breaking spiritual strongholds. Things in the unseen were being dismantled. Little did I know this was the fast that would also align me with God's plan for me and my family to move away from Russia, which was my home, and to the US. There were many strongholds to deal with in that move, but through that fast, I know that God was fighting my battles.

When I started that tour, I was 82 kilograms, or 181 pounds. I started the tour on the 28th day of fasting. Generally, during this kind of fast, a person loses weight every day. Through the entire tour, I was quoting Psalm 54:4 at least 100 times a day. "My God helps me and sustains me." The New Living Translation says, "The Lord keeps me alive." I like that one.

During that fast, it sometimes felt like I was fighting for my life. Considering the amount of energy I was exerting during the worship night and the daily travel, I thought I was for sure losing weight every day. So when I got home after the tour and weighed myself, I expected to be at 75 kilos or 165 pounds or less—but to my amazement, I had not lost one pound during the tour!

God had literally sustained my weight. I believe that my *enduo* moment in the green room, when I felt a supernatural adrenaline go through my body, balanced my bodily systems and caused me not to lose weight so I could finish what God had ordained me to do. I can't prove this, but this what I believe. It is a fact that I lost no weight in 10 days on an all-water fast.

All of this reinforces Jesus' teaching. When you are praying in the unseen, God will reward you openly. In that tour, I never got up on stage and announced my fast. If I had done that, the Bible says that I would have had my reward in full and that I would have been acting just like a hypocrite. But I kept my focus on the Lord, drawing strength from Him and keeping that sacrifice of worship unseen before men. As a result, the Lord not only preserved me during that fast, but He also prepared the path before me.

A NEW WINESKIN

Throughout the Bible in both Old and New Testaments, we find accounts of men and women who fasted for various reasons. When Jesus said in Matthew 6 that we are not to be like the hypocrites when we fast, He went on to explain how we should position our hearts with humility. But Jesus also taught us "why" we should fast.

One day as I was searching out specifically what Jesus had to say about fasting, a passage in Luke 5 that I have often wondered about was suddenly illuminated to me.

In Luke 5, we see that the Pharisees confronted Jesus, wanting to know why His disciples did not fast.

Then they said to Him, "Why do the disciples of John fast often and make prayers, and likewise those of the Pharisees, but Yours eat and drink?"

And He said to them, "Can you make the friends of the bridegroom fast while the bridegroom is with them? But the days will come when the bridegroom will be taken away from them; then they will fast in those days."

Luke 5:33-35 NKJV

That seemed clear enough. Jesus was saying that while He was on earth with His disciples, they did not need to fast because His presence with them was their access to the Father and the answer to their questions. But then Jesus gave a parable that was the key to unlock the spiritual significance of fasting:

He told them this parable: "No one tears a piece out of a new garment to patch an old one. Otherwise, they will have torn the new garment, and the patch from the new will not match the old. And no one pours new wine into old wineskins. Otherwise, the new wine will burst the skins; the wine will run out and the wineskins will be ruined. No, new wine must be poured into new wineskins. And no one after drinking old wine wants the new, for they say, 'The old is better.'"

Luke 5:36-39

Initially I didn't see the connection between this verse in the parable and fasting. What did a wineskin have to do with fasting? But when I asked the Lord about the meaning of it, He opened my understanding with the revelation that fasting has a key role in making us into a new wineskin.

A new wineskin is not something we possess; a new wineskin is something we become. Only new wineskins are capable of being containers of the new wine, which is the fresh outpouring of God's Spirit.

To become a new wineskin starts with a choice that unfolds into an ongoing process of yielding and a continual expression of surrender and consecration. If that yielding stops, the wineskin ceases to become new. With no capacity to hold the new wine, the person who chooses to remain an old wineskin will prefer "the old wine." In other words, if there is no hunger to pursue God and press in for a life without limits, a person will settle for a life with limits and conclude that a comfortable, unchallenged lifestyle will do.

That description of an old wineskin resembles the traits of a person who does not hunger for God's Word or thirst to pursue His presence. That person has no real capacity to receive the outpouring of the Spirit, which is the "new wine." Instead of humbling himself to yield and respond to the movement of God's Spirit, aligning with the changes He requires of each believer, the person who chooses to remain an old wineskin will prefer "the old wine."

What begins as an unwillingness to yield to God eventually hardens into an inability to respond or even recognize what He is doing.

That was the case with the hypocrites Jesus rebuked. Their pride and pursuit of the praise of men hardened their hearts and made them incapable of recognizing the Messiah when He stood before them. They didn't just fail to recognize who Jesus was; they were offended by Him. Instead of embracing Jesus, they clung to the traditions of men. As a result, they missed the time of their visitation and wasted the opportunity they had been given.

THE POWER OF A FASTED LIFE

Living a fasted lifestyle develops an increasing hunger for God even more than specific periods of fasting. Fasting is not what moves God. Your *faith* moves God. But fasting moves you into a position of humility that subdues your flesh as you surrender to God. And when you draw near to God with that posture of heart, God draws near to you.

A life that is daily devoted to walking yielded before God in this way will be endowed with power to continually release a greater manifestation of His presence. And it is the presence and power of God that changes everything.

The Lord told me that He viewed my life as a living prayer during that time of extended fasting. It wasn't because I was going without food that He received my life as a prayer and a sacrifice. It was because of my posture of yielded dependence upon Him.

Every day I acknowledged God as my strength and my wisdom. I laid aside my will for His, and His Word became more necessary to me than natural food.

That is the posture of a fasted life—a lifestyle of pursuit, a lifestyle of worship, a lifestyle of deliberately laying aside the desires of self to seek His. And, yes, that includes times of fasting that keep the spirit sensitive and clear while silencing the voice of the flesh and its appetites.

MY PRAYER

Father, thank You for teaching me that fasting is all about humility. I understand that Jesus said hypocrites brag to others that they are fasting and pray about themselves. You taught us that people who do that have their reward in full. By Your grace and with Your help, Father, I will not be a hypocrite; I choose Your way. I choose humility. I will keep my fasting as secret as possible, because I understand that what is unseen is rewarded by You. Most of all, instead of praying for myself and my needs, I will worship You and pray for others. You already know my needs, so there's no need for me to beg for what I have already received. Jesus, You chose the Cross. You chose humility, and I will do the same. Lord, help me live a life of continual surrender to You so I can be a new wineskin, filled to overflowing with the power and the presence of Your Spirit. In the name of Jesus I pray. Amen.

CHAPTER 5

SONSHIP: THE POSTURE OF A FASTED LIFE

THE PURPOSE OF a fasted life is to become a new wineskin capable of being filled continually with the new wine of the Holy Spirit.

This ability to be a new wineskin, filled with the fullness of God, is available to all of His children so they can manifest His glory on the earth. But only those who choose to live vitally united to God by a lifestyle of surrender will experience the kind of close communion that results in a bold demonstration of His power on the earth.

Those who press in on purpose to become intimately acquainted with God through worship, prayer, and His Word will know their God and be strong to do exploits. They will manifest their sonship by their consistent, deliberate pursuit of His presence and their obedience to fulfill His desires and not their own—because they will know His ways, not just His acts.

Fasting is a vital part of this process. It shifts you to a posture of humility, which is necessary to move into true intimacy with the Father. From that posture, you will enter into alignment with God, which will enable you to access His heart. And when you move into alignment with God, His hand is released to move on your behalf.

The Posture and the Position

So humility is the posture of a fasted life, and sonship is its position. A fasted lifestyle is a product of our relationship with the Father, which is fueled by time with Him in His Word, in worship, and in prayer as an expression of our love and continual hunger for Him. Periods of fasting and prayer are expressions of worship that carry weight in the Spirit when they are released from the position of a son or daughter honoring the Father versus the position of a servant begging a master.

> *When you pray, don't babble on and on as the Gentiles do. They think their prayers are answered merely by repeating their words again and again. Don't be like them, for your Father knows exactly what you need even before you ask him!*
>
> Matthew 6:7-8 NLT

This is a powerful scripture. Jesus is not only speaking about our motivation in prayer, but He is also addressing our identification as sons. When we view ourselves as servants who need to convince God to do something or to give us something, we are operating out of a consumer mentality instead of a Kingdom mindset. We come to Him for something He can do for us.

But God, being a true Father, wants us to come to Him because of who He is to us and who we are in Him—sons and daughters. As His children, our praying should not babble on about what we want or need, like the world does. Our relationship with God is not about getting something; it is all about giving Him all that we are because He has already given us everything.

At different times, people have questioned me about why I am fasting: "Did something horrible happen to you? What tragedy has happened? What are you believing for God to do?" My reply is always, "Everything is great!"

Why should I fast to get something? Why should I fast for a breakthrough? My motive is not for God to bail me out. My motive is to bless my God. He's my Father, and I want to pour my love on Him.

My daughters don't have to do something special to impress me. They know I love them. Many times they wake up in the morning and come find me just to hug me. This blesses me so much that I want to give them something. I may say, "Let's go get some ice cream. Today's breakfast is ice cream!" With that one hug, I am ready to break all the rules. I am ready to do the unexpected just to bless them. I react like this because my daughters' motive is just to love me with no strings attached.

We all want to be appreciated for who we are, not just sought out for what we can do. For example, we all like it when someone takes us out to lunch, but we don't like to later realize that the only reason that person took us to lunch was to get something from us. This personally turns me off, and I most likely won't meet with that person again because their motive was to get something from me.

Have you ever called someone to say, "How are you? How is your day going?"

That person may reply, "Doing well. How can I help you?"

You answer, "I don't want anything. You were just on my heart. I wanted to tell you that you're a blessing, and I hope you have an awesome day! That's it!"

People will usually be surprised and then feel very blessed. You have won their hearts simply by caring about them and not calling to get something from them. At that point, they will be delighted to serve you at a time when you possibly do need their help. You made their day by just saying hello. You won their hearts!

We touch and bless the heart of God when we come to Him in simple love, just to be with Him. It's then that we find His hand move on our behalf, perfecting what concerns us.

A HIGHER LEVEL OF FASTING

A posture of humility, worshiping the Lord for who He is while also acknowledging our deep need for Him, is the posture of a fasted lifestyle.

If you don't receive specific guidance from the Lord, you get to choose your motive for a particular fast. Are you fasting and praying with a specific reason in mind? Are you fasting to receive direction? Are you fasting for financial breakthrough? Are you fasting to get healed? Are you fasting for your family to be strong? Are you fasting for family members or friends to get saved?

These are all good desires. But if you are fasting and praying just to get something from God without pressing in to know Him more intimately, you may get what you are asking for, but your relationship with Him will not grow. In fact, you will most likely find yourself in the same situation again because you held yourself in the position of a consumer. A consumer relationship is based on a "point of purchase" approach: "I'll scratch your back and you scratch mine! I'll give you something if you give me something in return."

This type of transactional situation took place between God and the Israelites many times. They would pray to God when they were in trouble; then God would hear them and save them. But because they had no consistency in their relationship with God, they would repeat the same cycle again and again. We see this pattern repeated in Psalm 107:13,19,28 (KJV):

> *Then they cried unto the Lord in their trouble, and he saved them out of their distresses. ...Then they cry unto the Lord in their trouble, and he saveth them out of their distresses. ...Then they cry unto the Lord in their trouble, and he bringeth them out of their distresses.*

This is what the Israelites did time and time again, and it never got them anywhere.

But before we start judging the children of Israel, we need to take a look at our own hearts and lives. You and I have done the exact same thing; there is nothing new under the sun. Just like the Israelites, we have sought God's hand but not His heart.

On the other hand, when we humble ourselves and draw near to God through fasting—to seek Him and to know His heart without a consumer mindset—He will take care of all our needs without our even begging for it. When we touch His heart, His hand will move.

Just like my daughters win my heart with a hug that makes me want to do anything for them, our Heavenly Father's heart is won in the same way. By fasting with the right motive, I cause my relationship with God to reflect a degree of intimacy that deepens, and He answers all of my needs without my asking for anything.

Our Heavenly Father already knows all of our needs, so we don't need to beg Him for anything. We just need to spend time with Him, worship Him, and act on His Word. Our motive is not to babble on about our needs in vain repetition, as Jesus said in Matthew 6:7. Our motive is just to worship and to love Him. We seek His heart, not His hand!

When you worship our Heavenly Father like this, you are operating in a higher level of faith in your fasting. In addition, your life will reflect a higher level of authority because of your deepening level of intimacy with Him.

CAN WE MOVE GOD?

I have stated many times in this book that fasting does not move God. Fasting and praying causes you to be aligned with God's perfect will for your life. Let's remember what Romans 12:1 says—you become a living sacrifice, and this brings you into a greater knowledge of His perfect will for your life. This is your reasonable service. God does not change, so you can't change His mind. You can't move God through fasting, but you can move yourself into alignment with God's plan for your life.

As I was explaining this point to one of my friends, he said, "I get what you are saying about how God cannot be moved, but what about Moses? Moses pleaded with God, and God changed His mind or intention."

The Scripture passage that my friend was referring to is found in Exodus 32:9-14 (NKJV):

> *And the Lord said to Moses, "I have seen this people, and indeed it is a stiff-necked people! Now therefore, let Me alone, that My wrath may burn hot against them and I may consume them. And I will make of you a great nation."*
>
> *Then Moses pleaded with the Lord his God, and said: "Lord, why does Your wrath burn hot against Your people whom You have brought out of the land of Egypt with great power and with a mighty hand? Why should the Egyptians speak, and say, 'He brought them out to harm them, to kill them in the mountains, and to consume them from the face of the earth'? Turn from Your fierce wrath, and relent from this harm to Your people. Remember Abraham, Isaac, and Israel, Your servants, to whom You swore by Your own self, and said to them, 'I will multiply your descendants as the stars of heaven; and all this land that I*

have spoken of I give to your descendants, and they
shall inherit it forever.'" So the Lord relented from
the harm which He said He would do to His people.

Interestingly, in this situation it would seem that God's mind was changed, because He did not destroy the people of Israel. In the New Living Translation, verse 14 states, *"So the Lord changed his mind about the terrible disaster he had threatened to bring on his people."*

So it does seem that you can move God, and maybe you can even change His mind.

I paused for a moment as I talked with my friend. As I thought about it, I realized that Moses did not move God, and God did not change His mind. Rather, God was testing His relationship with Moses. God verbalized His displeasure with the people to set the stage for a very provocative discussion. Then He watched to see how Moses would react. I personally believe that this situation was a test of Moses' faith and of the depth of his relationship with God.

Let me give you an example from my own life as a parent. One day my oldest daughter walked up to me and my wife and asked, "Dad and Mom, can you buy me some paint materials so I can paint?"

Our reply was, "No, you can believe God for that."

Although as parents, we could have bought our daughter paint materials, we chose to say no so that she would learn to put her trust in God to grant her the desires of her heart.

Sure enough, our daughter prayed and someone blessed her with materials to paint with. When her parents said no, a situation was set up that caused her faith to grow when she received her desire.

Our reply also tested our relationship with our daughter. She could have gotten upset or offended and said, "Now I'll never be able to paint because I don't have the materials." Instead, she decided to trust God—and He came through for her!

Praise the Lord! God came through for Moses, and He came through for my daughter. I'm confident God will come through for you too!

Just as our answer caused our daughter to grow in her faith, God's answer to Moses caused Moses' faith to grow.

Would Moses say, "Okay, God. Kill them! They deserve it"? Or would he say, "God, You said that You would save Your people and make them a mighty nation. How will they be a mighty nation if You kill them all right now?"

God was testing Moses to see if he would respond according to God's character and quote God's words back to Him.

We find another example of this kind of test in the New Testament. Interestingly enough, Jesus did the same thing. He said something that could have provoked great anger, but it provoked great faith instead. Even Jesus marveled at the response He received. Let's take a look:

> *And behold, a woman who was a Canaanite from*
> *that district came out and, with a [loud, trouble-*
> *somely urgent] cry, begged, Have mercy on me, O*
> *Lord, Son of David! My daughter is miserably and*

distressingly and cruelly possessed by a demon! But He did not answer her a word. And His disciples came and implored Him, saying, Send her away, for she is crying out after us. He answered, I was sent only to the lost sheep of the house of Israel. But she came and, kneeling, worshiped Him and kept praying, Lord, help me! And He answered, It is not right (proper, becoming, or fair) to take the children's bread and throw it to the little dogs.

She said, Yes, Lord, yet even the little pups (little whelps) eat the crumbs that fall from their [young] masters' table. Then Jesus answered her, O woman, great is your faith! Be it done for you as you wish. And her daughter was cured from that moment.

Matthew 15:22-28 AMPC

Such a strange, even controversial story! A woman was following Jesus, screaming, "My daughter is demon-possessed. Please heal her!" But Jesus just kept walking and didn't acknowledge her cries. She continued shouting at Jesus as He ignored her. Then the woman called Him the Son of David, acknowledging that He was the Messiah.

When Jesus finally spoke to her, He said, "I am called to the Israelites, and you are a Canaanite. It's not right to take the children's bread and give it to the dogs."

It would seem that Jesus was acting rude toward the Canaanite woman by not taking heed to her pleas. Then on top of that, Jesus called her a dog—which is how the Jews of that day commonly referred to the mixed lineage of the Canaanites. The conversation seemed to go from bad to worse!

Everything about this scenario seems contrary to the compassionate character of Jesus. The disciples were probably shocked and wondering: What happened to our loving Jesus? But then came the statement from the Canaanite woman that shocked Jesus.

In response to Jesus' calling her a dog, the Canaanite woman boldly replied: "True, but even the little dogs eat the crumbs from their master's table." She didn't even attempt to refute what He said. But she did refuse to accept His denial—which is exactly the point Jesus was making in Matthew 7:7 when He said, "Keep on asking; keep on knocking; and the closed door will open."

This woman's response got Jesus' attention! He exclaimed that she had great faith, essentially saying to her, "Woman, your faith is huge! Your situation will be exactly as you've desired!"

What was Jesus doing when He ignored the Canaanite woman and then even told her she didn't qualify to receive what she was crying out to receive from Him? He was not being rude. Jesus knew exactly what He was doing. According to the Old Covenant, He spoke the truth. This woman didn't qualify for the children's bread of healing. But He also knew that faith would supersede that. If she believed, she would receive.

Jesus knew that His actions intensified the woman's pursuit, stimulated her faith, and caused the strength of her expectation to lay hold of her breakthrough. And notice how Jesus complimented her: "Oh woman, great is your faith! Be it done as you wish." And immediately her own faith secured what she needed.

This Canaanite woman's passionate pursuit, her heartfelt worship of Jesus, and her unrelenting persistence demonstrated that she believed Jesus was good and that He would do good toward her tormented daughter. Possessing the needed humility to push past feeling first ignored and then insulted, this woman's faith in the Son of God brought her into perfect alignment with His character and His will—to do good to all. Her own faith touched the heart of Jesus and secured her daughter's deliverance because she believed that He was good and powerful. She believed one crumb was all she needed, and by faith she took it.

SON OR SERVANT?

So what do you believe about God's character? What do you believe about yourself?

Jesus had not gone to the Cross or been raised from the dead when the Canaanite women cried out to Him in fervent pursuit. But now a covenant with God through Jesus Christ is available to Jew and Gentile alike. Whosoever will believe can become a child of God and eat from the Master's table.

God desires each one of us to accept His invitation to become the sons and the daughters of God. After you accept that invitation, it's your choice whether you embrace and put on your identity in Christ and walk in the position of a son that is yours through Jesus. Even if you are a son, how you see yourself—as a servant or a son—will determine the quality of your relationship with God. That's why it's important to align yourself with Him and to see yourself as He sees you.

That's an area in which I struggled for years. But it was during a time of drawing near to God in fasting that He opened my understanding to the revelation of my identity as a son versus a servant. It changed my life completely. I want to share those simple yet profound insights with you. Because I believe understanding that we are sons—not beggarly servants—is the posture of a fasted life and the basis of understanding our authority in Christ.

When Jesus died on the Cross, He paid the full penalty of sin that separated us from God. Then when God resurrected Jesus from the dead, He raised us up together with Him in victory to be united with Him in Christ. This positioned us for greatness to rule and reign with Him in the heavenly realms in Christ Jesus.

> *But God—so rich is He in His mercy! Because of and in order to satisfy the great and wonderful and intense love with which He loved us, even when we were dead (slain) by [our own] shortcomings and trespasses, He made us alive together in fellowship and in union with Christ; [He gave us the very life of Christ Himself, the same new life with which He quickened Him, for] it is by grace (His favor and mercy which you did not deserve) that you are saved (delivered from judgment and made partakers of Christ's salvation). And He raised us up together with Him and made us sit down together [giving us joint seating with Him]*

in the heavenly sphere [by virtue of our being] in
Christ Jesus (the Messiah, the Anointed One).

Ephesians 2:4-6 AMPC

Christ positioned us to be seated with Him, but we can hold on to beliefs that hinder us and cause us not to function in our seat of authority. Sin, of course, can cause us to miss the mark. Our motives can also cause us to miss the mark when we pray.

An example of a wrong motive while fasting is to pray to see miracles without seeking to know the God of miracles. Seeking His hand but not His heart is the position of a beggar, which is not our identity in Christ.

On the other hand, when you fast and pray with the motive to know the heart and mind of God and to align with Him on a matter, that approach immediately positions you correctly before your Heavenly Father. In that position, you are not approaching Him as a beggar; rather, your approach is confident and honoring. You are walking in your authority as a son in the house of our Father God.

ACTING LIKE A SON OF THE HOUSE

When Ella and I and our children were still living in Russia, there was a time when a passage in the book of Romans was burning in my heart for several weeks. It seemed that God wouldn't let me read anything else but this scripture.

For you did not receive the spirit of slavery to fall
back into fear, but you have received the Spirit of
adoption as sons, by whom we cry, "Abba! Father!"
Romans 8:15 ESV

I was also impressed to fast off and on during that entire time, so I knew that God was trying to tell me something. Then one day I was struck with a strong desire for God to show me what it meant to be a son in His house. That day it was all I could think about. Through His Word, He was planting a desire within me for the revelation that would be the key to opening my understanding of my identity in Him. That insight would change everything and unlock a deeper experience in my relationship with Him.

The next day after I had expressed my desire to the Lord to know what it meant to be a son in His house, I had a significant encounter that showed me what the confident expectation of a son looked like. My wife asked me to go to the store and gave me $5 to buy some bread and milk. When I put the $5 in my pocket, I discovered I had an extra $100 that I didn't know was there. We were living in Russia at that time, and $100 was a lot of money! This was $100 that my wife knew nothing about. I was excited because I wanted to do something nice for my wife. She deserved it. This was an opportunity to buy her a gift that would be a total surprise.

Right before I walked into the store to buy bread, I saw a little girl, who looked about 12 years old, begging for money. I thought to myself, *I wish I could help.*

Then I heard Holy Spirit say, "Philip, you can do something. Remember the $100 in your pocket?"

I thought, *No, that's for my special gift to Ella.*

Then I walked into the store, bought our milk and bread, and was on the way out the door. The young girl was still there begging. I thought to myself again, *I wish I could help.* Then I heard that still small voice getting louder: "Philip, you can help. Remember the 100 dollars?" At that point, my flesh was screaming, "The $100 is for Ella!" But the voice of the Holy Spirit persisted in my spirit. Finally, I submitted.

I walked up to the girl and said, "I would like to buy you some groceries. You can have anything you want!" Those are extremely dangerous words to tell a 12-year-old. She nodded; then she walked into the store and confidently got a grocery cart. This kind of scared me because in my mind I was planning to spend maybe an extra ten dollars. But when she got the shopping cart, I realized this was not going to go the way I planned.

As girl walked in the store, she chose the most expensive milk, bread, fruit, candy, rice, and other items. It did not take long before her cart was completely full. She was walking down the aisles, grabbing stuff off the shelves as fast as she could.

I realized very quickly that my $100 was barely going to cut it, so I asked her to stop. She looked at me like I was her worst enemy. Obviously, she had intended to buy even more! When we checked out, the bill was exactly $100 dollars to the cent!

I didn't know it at the time, but God was giving me the lesson I had requested just the day before.

At that time of the year, Moscow was cold and snow was everywhere. I did not want the girl to slip, so I offered to help carry her grocery bags to her apartment building. They looked heavy even for me as a grown man, so I knew that they were heavy for her. She looked at me and said, "No, these are mine." She was determined that they were not going to be taken from her.

So I asked, "May I at least walk you to your apartment building in case you need help?" The girl agreed.

As we walked, I saw that this girl didn't look like a beggar. She had a warm new coat, a pair of warm snow boots, and a nice woolen scarf. When we finally came to her apartment building, she thanked me and said goodbye.

Before I turned to leave, I had to ask the girl something. "You don't look like a beggar," I said, "so why are you begging?"

The girl's answer shocked me. She said, "My father is in prison, and my mom just had a baby so she can't work. She has to take care of the baby and my other siblings, and we needed food, so I decided to take care of my family." Then she walked into her apartment building.

With tears in my eyes, I stood there dumbfounded, in awe of her bravery. In that moment I realized just how close I had come to ignoring her. I had almost missed a wonderful opportunity to cooperate with God to make a positive impact on someone's life! It made me wonder how many times the still small voice of His Spirit had spoken to me, yet I had missed it because I was too preoccupied with myself.

Then I heard the Holy Spirit's voice in my spirit: "Philip, what that young girl did is how a son acts in My house."

Suddenly I remembered that that was the thought going through my head all week when I was reading Romans over and over again. I had been saying, "I am no longer a slave to fear; I am a child of God. Lord, show me how a son acts in Your house."

That meditation and declaration was working on my sense of identity—how I saw myself.

Holy Spirit asked me, "What did you tell the girl?"

"I told her she could have anything that she wanted."

"That's right. And here's what I am telling you, Philip: My Word is like that store. You can have anything in it that you want. Every good thing is in there, and it's all for you. Confidently and boldly receive it from Me just as that young girl received your offer to buy the groceries she wanted. This is the way a son acts in My house."

At that time, I was fasting at least one day a week, sometimes two. I say that only to indicate that I was deliberately making a practice of missing meals in order to silence my flesh and yield to the Lord. I was intentionally cultivating a spiritual habit of surrender to His Word and to His voice. As a result, my spirit was open, and that is how I was able to hear His voice that day.

Servant or Son Mindset

I went home that day and immediately began searching through the Scriptures to discover the differences between the mindset of a son and that of a servant. Here is what I found:

1. A household servant has no rights within the family he serves. A son has rights and benefits from his relationship in the family.

A servant no rights and no family standing in the house he serves. He has no rightful expectation of provision and no sense of belonging to a family unit that offers any type of assurance. A son, however, has love-based, fearless access to privileges because of his family name and heritage. We are no longer slaves to fear; we are the children of the Most High. We carry the name of Jesus that is above all other names. As Christians, as sons and daughters in God's family, we have the seal of the Holy Spirit.

> *And you also were included in Christ when you heard the message of truth, the gospel of your salvation. When you believed, you were marked in him with a seal, the promised Holy Spirit.*
>
> Ephesians 1:13

Sealed by the Power of the Name

When the enemy sees that seal of the Spirit on our lives, he understands that this means we are off-limits. He cannot conquer God's family. That seal represents the family name. And like the signet of a king, it represents power and authority that cannot be broken or disregarded. If a person tampers with the king's seal, it is viewed as an assault in opposition to his power. There will be immediate and harsh consequences to all violators—which his mighty armies will enforce.

There is so much power in that family name. Proverbs 18:10 (NASB) states, "The name of the Lord is a strong tower; the righteous runs into it and is safe." It doesn't say they lean on the tower; it says they run into it.

That means we're to get in the tower! Kenneth Copeland says we are in God's family, and we're in the name of Jesus. God's mighty name is a strong tower. The name of Jesus, the righteous Son of God, is our identity because He gave it to us.

You are not a slave; you are in the family and in the name of Jesus. You've been bought with His blood, redeemed from the curse of the Law, and sealed with His protection through His family name. You have been adopted into the family, and everything Father God has is yours.

2.   A servant may not exercise free will in his master's house, but a son has free will to make choices.

A household servant is not invited to express his opinions or aspirations. The only expectation is for him to do as told when he is told. This is a screenshot of a servant's life. A son, however, is expected to dream and to make choices that honor the legacy of his family.

Free will is a powerful weapon in our hands. We have the freedom to choose. The Bible clearly states that as sinners, we had no choice but to sin because our sin nature controlled us. But now, because of the Cross, we are free. We can choose to live our lives in alignment with God or contrary to His ways. God respects our choice. He doesn't always agree with our choices, but He respects our right to make them—a right that He gave us. God did not make us robots bound to obey our master and programmed to respond in only one way.

In giving us the privilege and the power of choice, God proved His love and faith. God wants us to follow Him because we love Him, not because we are forced to. Let's take reading the Word as an example.

For me personally, I make a choice every day to read the Word or ignore it. There is nothing on the inside of me that will force me to read the Word. Holy Spirit will gently nudge me and remind me to spend time with Him, but the nudge or whisper is so subtle that I can miss it easily. God wants to me to read the Word, not because I am forced to but because I made the decision to do so. I do this because I love Him.

Another example of this is seen in the home. A husband can make demands of his wife and the wife will follow him mostly because of fear of reprisal, but this kind of relationship will not be a satisfying one. There is, however, another approach. By the husband serving the wife and helping with chores, kids, and responsibilities around the house, a much stronger foundation is built that will last. Then when the time comes for the wife to follow the husband's advice when is it uncomfortable or costly but the right thing to do, she will follow not because she is forced to but because she loves and trusts her husband.

This is the way I lead my household—not with an iron fist but with a serving heart. Jesus said we must be the servant of all. I am by no means perfect. Holy Spirit is teaching me every day. But these are some principles that He has taught me over the years. I know that my wife followed me from Russia to America not only because she is an amazing woman of God, but also because of this strong principle of servanthood in our household.

Christ served us through His death on the Cross; therefore, we love Him because He first loved us. We follow Him not because we are forced to do so but because we love Him. A son has been graced with this powerful weapon of free will, so let us choose wisely to build the Kingdom of God.

3. A servant has no anticipated inheritance in the family, but a son receives an inheritance.

A servant has no anticipation of inheritance in the family. A son understands that he has access to everything in the house because it belongs to his father. A son never wonders if it is okay to get something out of the refrigerator in the house of his father. As servant wouldn't dare to help himself freely to his master's goods.

The liberty of the father gives liberty to the son. These are the same words that Jesus spoke about Himself: "When you see Me, you see the Father" (*see* John 14:9). Jesus was empowered and authorized by His Father. There was one heart, one mind, and one purpose in both the Father and Son.

This is a beautiful picture of unity. It is also an example of the way a son can walk in the inheritance of his father. We must do the same regarding the inheritance we have received from our Father God through Jesus Christ.

Through the Cross, Jesus gave us access to salvation, healing, grace, redemption, favor and prosperity, supernatural power, Holy Spirit, praying in the Spirit, authority, and dominion. We are more than conquerors through Him (Jesus) who loved us (*see* Rom. 8:37). All of this has been given to us through the great sacrifice that Jesus paid on the Cross. This is the great inheritance that is ours as sons and daughters in the house of God.

We are called to rule and reign as kings upon the earth, exercise dominion, and take authority over the works of darkness.

> *And you have caused them to become a Kingdom of priests for our God. And they will reign on the earth.*
>
> Revelation 5:10 NLT

We did not receive this inheritance just for ourselves. We received it for the building of the Kingdom of God. The Bible says that it is more blessed to give than to receive (*see* Acts 20:35). Everything that we received as our inheritance through the Cross we are to give away in service to the world for the purpose of bringing in God's great harvest.

4. A servant receives no mercy, but a son always receives mercy.

I grew up in a healthy, godly, but strict home. Sometimes my father would be told that he was too strict on us. Some would say that too much was required of us.

One day my dad took me aside and asked me, "Do you think I am too strict?"

My response was, "Dad you are strict, but I know that it is because you love me."

He replied, "Yes! Philip, you must understand that you are my future, and although I am strict, I am also forgiving. No matter how many times you mess up, I will do everything I can to support you again. I love you!"

Although Dad was strict, we also had fun with him. He would come home and spend quality time with us and take us on different ministry trips with him. We loved it.

Being a son is a big responsibility because you are a constant reflection of your father. The way you dress, talk, and act is in a constant state of scrutiny. Many times you feel like you are living in a glass house. Everyone is watching you.

As a pastor's son, this was my life. I was not permitted to dress the way others dressed. Movies that many others were allowed to watch were forbidden to me. The jokes that others might have laughed at were considered perverted and rude in my father's household. These rules and principles in our home were established to protect my spirit and to develop character and discipline—and I am very grateful for it today.

No family is perfect, and ours was no exception. Sometimes we got offended and had to ask forgiveness. Other times it was hard in the home because my dad traveled so much. Mom had to take care of the family in Dad's absence, especially when I was young. Many times we skipped vacation because the ministry schedule was too strenuous. Yet through all of this, I never felt neglected; I always felt like a part of the ministry and that we were building the Kingdom together as a family.

My father and mother instilled principles within me and my brothers that formed us into the men we are today.

Although we had difficult times, we also had greater times of victory. Through it all, I learned to represent my family the best I could because of all the love and knowledge that was passed down to me to ensure my future. In all of this, I learned how to grow in responsibility and how to be accountable for my actions.

I learned to imitate my parents so I could be a son who honored and reflected them. I emphasize this point because it reveals a scriptural truth:

> *Imitate God, therefore, in everything you do, because you are his dear children.*
>
> Ephesians 5:1 NLT

As believers, we are sons in the Kingdom. Even in the midst of pressure or difficulty, we must represent our Heavenly Father with holiness and honor. Although our Father is strict and has high standards and a narrow path for us to follow, in Him we have great love and mercy.

Our responsibility is to imitate our Heavenly Father. He will teach us to understand responsibility and accountability as we are faithful through each heavenly assignment He gives us. It is a great privilege to be a son in our Father's house.

This is a powerful truth that is definitely not the case for a servant. A servant receives no praise, regardless of what he accomplishes. If he has done what was requested, it is considered his reasonable service. In fact, he is scrutinized and punished if he fails to do what was required. Even when the assignment in done is a pristine manner, it might be judged at the whim of his master. There is no custom of benevolent mercy for a servant, only judgment.

5. A son evaluates himself according to the standards of his family. A servant evaluates himself according to his own accomplishments.

I think this is the hardest lesson of all. When I moved to the United States. I was following God's voice. I had no idea what to expect. All I knew was that it was time to go and God would prepare the way. In Russia I was ministering at least nine months out of the year; I was constantly on the go. But God told me to leave it all and go to America for revival.

America was a land I knew almost nothing about because I had been living in Russia for 25 years. God told me it would be a new season. I expected that it would mean increase because if you follow God's voice, blessing must be immediate—right? Wrong!

I was shocked when almost no one trusted me to preach. Pastors and ministers were very cautious about me. I am grateful for those who immediately trusted me, but it was not enough to fill a whole schedule. Most of the time I studied the Word and stayed home. This was actually a blessing because I needed time to build my marriage in the midst of such a drastic change. I also needed to spend more time with my children after their world had changed so completely. But the desire in me to go was screaming, "Do something!"

Everyone back home in Russia was asking me, "When are you returning home? Come back! Why did you move?"

I did at least six trips to that side of world the first year I was in America. Some lasted two weeks; some lasted longer. I ministered in Russia and the surrounding countries more than I did in America. Friends, ministers, family, and my own logical reasonings wondered out loud, *What was the point of me moving to America if I still minister in Russia all the time?*

I would conclude a trip, excited about what took place. But when I returned to Tulsa, it felt like a desert while I waited for the next ministry trip. All I did was study and pray, and I was grateful for Millennial Church that constantly strengthened me in my walk with God.

It was during this time that God instructed me again to fast. During the fast, I briefly went into a state of depression. I was constantly looking at what people were doing on the other side of the world. I would see my friends get invited to the conferences where I used to speak. I would watch their music and Instagram followers begin to grow while mine did not. Facebook and Instagram became a constant source of discouragement.

My mindset was completely wrong. I was measuring myself against what I used to do and comparing myself to all my friends, whose lives looked like they were thriving in ministry while I looked and felt stuck. The Bible is clear that those who measure themselves against themselves and compare themselves against others are not wise (*see* 2 Cor. 10:12). Admittedly, I was not acting very wisely at that point.

It was during this time that God revealed to me that my mindset was wrong. I was evaluating myself through what I did instead of on who I am in Him. My ministry had become my identity, and if I wasn't doing anything that I considered "ministry," I felt as though I had lost my identity and value.

I repented, and as I prayed and sought the Lord, He showed me that I had a servant mentality—but not in a good way. I was actually thinking like a slave, evaluating myself through what I did or what I had accomplished, whereas a son is confident because of who he is, not what he does. As I fasted and prayed, drawing near to the Father to know and to learn His ways, He revealed to me my value in His eyes—and when He did, it changed how I saw myself and everyone around me!

WE ARE GOD'S SPECIAL TREASURE!

Although we have received the treasure of an inheritance from God through the Cross of Christ, God considers us to be *His* special treasure and precious possession.

God, who owns all of the earth with all of its natural resources—who controls the universe and has all dominion and authority to control everything—considers you more valuable that all of that. I find it phenomenal that God calls us His special treasure.

> *For the Lord has chosen Jacob for Himself, Israel for His special treasure.*
> Psalm 135:4 NKJV

Humans—even in our fallen state, with all of our flaws and deficiencies—are called God's treasured possession or special treasure. It's a powerful statement, but what does it mean?

This is extremely hard to fathom, but here it is: You are more valuable to God than anything else in the universe. He gave His best for you. He gave Jesus, His only begotten Son.

God considered you worth fighting for. Wars are fought and families even separate over inheritances. That's right— you are God's special treasure and inheritance. A war was fought over you between God and the devil. When Jesus was resurrected on the third day, He won that war. He completely embarrassed and humiliated the enemy.

> *And having disarmed the powers and authorities, he made a public spectacle of them, triumphing over them by the cross.*
> Colossians 2:15

I am saying all of this to emphasize to you that you are valuable to God. You are His special treasure and inheritance.

YOU ARE VALUABLE!

This is the reason the devil opposes you so fiercely. He wants nothing more than to hurt God by stealing, killing, and ultimately destroying what is most valuable to Him—you!

As sons of God, you are created by Him to rule and reign. The Father is honored when you walk in your sonship, exercising your authority in Him and taking dominion. But Satan wants to dishonor God by deceiving you, distorting your perception of yourself so that you will think and act like slaves under his control instead of as the sons of God. When you see yourself other than how God sees you and created you to be, you will not experience the full purpose of God's intent for your life.

Other people are attached to your purpose. Your obedience will have an impact on their lives. If you have the mindset of a lowly beggar or servant and not a son, you will never reach for the dream that God created you to fulfill.

It hurts the Father to see His sons, for whom Christ died, live beneath their privilege. That privilege includes the opportunity to take responsibility in working with the Father to win souls into His Kingdom and to drive back the forces of darkness by the power of His Spirit.

From the start of Satan's rebellion that got him kicked out of Heaven, he wanted to exalt his rule above God's. This is exactly what he tried to do when he deceived Eve and enticed Adam to disobey God. Through sin, Satan took authority over God's most prized possession—man.

But God was not outmaneuvered! He had already prepared to send His Son Jesus as the last Adam to regain that authority through His death on the Cross.

God fought for you and won! You are valuable, and Satan fears your potential!

You Have Great Potential!

The devil does not want you to realize your value and your potential in God. Satan knows that once you understand the inheritance you carry as a son or daughter in the family of God, you will unleash against him the same mighty power that raised Jesus—because the same power that resurrected Jesus from the dead is on the inside of you (*see* Rom. 8:11)!

Understanding this truth will make you bold to walk and talk like your Father, which will destroy the enemy's plans. Then you will truly rule and reign as Jesus did on earth.

> *How God anointed Jesus of Nazareth with the Holy Spirit and power, and how he went around doing good and healing all who were under the power of the devil, because God was with him.*
>
> Acts 10:38

When God showed me that I had the wrong mindset, it actually set me free. Fear of man fell away because I realized that to find my sense of value from anything I did or from what people thought about what I did was too low. God sees me as valuable not because of my ministry or my accomplishments, or even because of my natural family. All of that is good, but He views me through the lens of His Word of God and His precious blood that was spilled for me on Calvary.

When I started to look at myself the way God looked at me, I changed and my family changed. Most importantly, my relationship with God changed, and I started speaking to Him with authority as a son in His house. It was only then that the opportunities and doors I had asked God to open up for revival began to open up.

The bottom line is this: Your identity is not in your ministry, church, or family. All of that can fail. I pray that doesn't happen, but you have to face the fact that you live in a real world with a real enemy who wants to destroy you. If your identity is in ministry, church, family, or job and they fail, then you fail as well.

So do yourself a favor: Evaluate yourself through something that will never fail. Evaluate yourself through the Word of God and the blood of Jesus. Make sure your focus is on Him and nothing else. Everything else can fail, but God alone is faithful.

> *The grass withers and the flowers fade, but the word of our God stands forever.*
>
> Isaiah 40:8 NLT

REVELATION AND UNDERSTANDING RECEIVED WHILE FASTING

Through fasting and prayer, the Lord revealed to me my mistaken sense of identity based on wrongly evaluating myself. There are many things that God wants to unravel before our eyes through fasting and prayer.

If you will be led by the Spirit in how and when to fast, God will grant revelation to you about many things. When you turn away from your own thoughts and the thoughts of the world around you, God will open the eyes of your understanding to recognize truths from His Word—truths you may have thought that you understood before, but you didn't fully grasp because they weren't activated and at work in your life.

Everything I have written in this chapter, I received during a season of fasting and praying that the Lord instructed me to do. That time of ministering to Him in fasting and prayer transformed my relationship with Him, with others, and even with myself. Through the truths He revealed to me that I just shared with you, I became better equipped to deal with the enemy.

This is the power that is made available to you as you make a decision to know God in a deeper way. The journey that God takes you on as you fast is an exciting one, but also one that will cause you grow through every storm. Your growth won't come because of the storm, but because of your dependence on His presence in the midst of difficulty.

You may wonder why I put so much emphasis on contrasting the mindset of a servant versus the mindset of a son. When we live in constant awareness of our sonship, we will walk in the righteousness that is ours through faith in Jesus Christ. This pleases the Father and honors the great sacrifice He made in sending Jesus as a Lamb to take away the sins of the world. By embracing the gift of sonship He gave us through Jesus, we strengthen our relationship with the Father, abiding vitally united with Him as we allow His truth to abide in us. From that place of obedient surrender, we will operate as one with Him. And as a result, we will bring glory to His name as we manifest His will and purpose on the earth.

MY PRAYER

Father, I thank You for teaching me that I am not a slave. I am a son/daughter of God. All of Your promises for me are yes and amen! Thank You that as a part of Your family, I carry all the family rights. I have free will. I have received a glorious inheritance because of the Cross. I can always come to the throne of grace to receive mercy. I evaluate myself not through the things of this world, but through Your Word and the blood of Jesus.

Thank You for teaching me to walk, talk, and act as a representative of Your family and Kingdom.

Thank You, Holy Spirit, for drawing me into a deeper level of intimacy with the Father. The earth is crying out for me to walk in my sonship to exercise dominion over all the works of the wicked one.

Father, I purpose to increasingly know You practically through experience for myself. Thank You for making me a new wineskin, filled to overflowing with new wine. Daily I set myself to receive a fresh outpouring of the Holy Spirit, and I am empowered daily to manifest Your goodness and Your glory. You make me strong to do exploits as I live to honor Your great name! You alone are worthy to be praised. In the name of Jesus I pray. Amen.

CHAPTER 6

SENSITIVITY TO HIS VOICE

Divine Intervention Results When God Calls You to Fast

I remember waking up one Sunday morning and hearing God's voice very strongly in my spirit: "You must fast today." I was actually discouraged by this because I had already fasted several times that week. I really wanted to eat, but I could not deny that there was a sense of urgency in the way He spoke to me. Not willingly, but obediently I said yes and went to church. That Sunday was a great day. All three services went wonderfully.

After the third service, my flesh started screaming, "Feed me! You sang three services. I need food before you lead worship for the youth service."

I thought to myself, *It's almost 5 o'clock. I have fasted almost the whole day. I can eat now!*

Then the sense of urgency rose up again as I heard in my spirit, "Don't do it! Fast!"

I recognized the urgency, but I was not very enthusiastic about it because I was hungry! I even went to the church cafeteria and looked at the food. People offered to buy my food because they could tell I was hungry.

I began to rationalize within myself, *Well, people are offering me food, so that must be a sign that my fast is over.*

Your flesh will always tell you what you want to hear, but your spirit will always lead you to follow the Holy Spirit's direction, whether you understand why or not.

As I was about to take a bite of a sandwich and break my fast, I felt that sense of urgency stop me again: "Fast!" A little upset and very hungry, I put the sandwich down and went to the sound check for the youth service.

My wife came in and registered our oldest daughter Mia for her service in the children's department. Everything was good. It had been a great day. In my mind, I wondered, *Why I was so stirred to fast?* I knew that it would be very possible that I would never know.

When you yield to a fasted lifestyle, you become sensitive to draw near to Him at His request, not just by your own desire. Your prayer then becomes multi-dimensional, taking on a strength and focus that He knows needs to be applied.

You might be praying just because God wants you to spend time with Him. And although you are going about your day, fulfilling other duties, that time of fasting is a deeply focused fellowship as you choose to arrest the cravings of your flesh and treasure Him more than your necessary food (*see* Job 23:12). God might be prompting you to pray with fasting because someone is in danger. In that case, your fast becomes a spiritual weapon that applies pressure against spiritual forces attempting to do harm. Or it could be all of the above at the same time!

Sometimes when God tells you to pray, you will never know the reason why. But if His Spirit is telling you to fast and draw near, there is a reason. So be sensitive and obedient to His voice. In doing this, you are praying out the perfect will of the Father.

As I continued with the sound check, everything seemed great. Suddenly to my surprise, the girl who was taking care of my two-year-old daughter during sound check came running to the front of the stage. Her face was filled with fear as she said to me, "Pastor, you have to go to your daughter right now! She is choking, and her face is blue. She choked on a cookie, and it's stuck in her throat. Mia can't breathe!"

As the girl said those words, something amazing happened. Instead of being overcome with feelings of worry, fear, and anxiety, I felt total and complete peace. The girl urged me to come quickly. I simply replied, "Mia will be fine. All is well; don't worry."

She looked at me with a confused expression and said, "Okay."

In less than a minute, she came back with excitement and said, "Don't worry. Mia is fine. The cookie came out of her throat!"

I looked at her and simply replied, "God is so good."

I don't know exactly when the cookie came out and my daughter stopped choking. But I do know that my not giving in to fear, anxiety, and worry was vital in that moment. The peace and calm of God that enveloped me was supernatural. I know if I had been in fear, words of unbelief could have hindered God working in that situation.

The truth is, if I had not been fasting that day, I don't know if my faith would have been that strong. Choosing to be obedient to the sense of urgency in my spirit to fast was an expression of faith. I trusted that the Lord was leading me, whether I understood why or not. My obedience to fast required faith and surrender of my will to His, and it kept me positioned in a place of yielded connection to His power and His presence. God knew that would be necessary. My obedient surrender to fast became an access point for Him to give me a miracle I didn't know I needed.

Afterward, the children's director walked up to me and said, "Philip, in ten years I have never seen anything like this."

I replied, "All is well. God is fighting for us."

She was shocked and replied, "God knew all of this would happen."

I replied "Yes, He did."

The Bible tells us that God goes before us to prepare the way and fight for us (see Deut. 31:8). But that does not exclude our involvement. Our faith and obedience are an expression of our will to invite Him to work in our situations. I don't know what would have happened if I had not been fasting that day. All I know is that in my weakness, His strength was made perfect in me.

As I leaned and relied upon Him during that fast, not knowing why the prompting was so urgent, my faith in Him was strengthened and nothing could move me. I believe that when I told the girl watching my two-year-old daughter that all was well, that was actually the gift of faith being activated in me by the grace of God. I believe that was the point of breakthrough. It was at that moment I had perfect peace, although the situation was shouting for a much different response.

BE ALERT!

One of the things that happens as you fast is you become very sensitive to the prompting of the Holy Spirit. When the voice of your flesh is quieted down, you can hear God's voice more clearly. As you fast, you become alert to God's voice and His direction for your life. Fasting does not cause God to speak to you; it simply clears away all the distractions and "noise" so that you can hear Him speak to you. Your spirit tunes in to His frequency, and the static of the world and your own flesh are tuned out. The truth is, God is speaking to you constantly; you just aren't hearing Him.

> *Yet now be strong, alert, and courageous, O Zerubbabel, says the Lord; be strong, alert, and courageous, O Joshua son of Jehozadak, the high priest; and be strong, alert, and courageous, all you people of the land, says the Lord, and work! For I am with you, says the Lord of hosts.*
>
> Haggai 2:4 AMPC

Now more than ever, the Body of Christ must be more alert. If God wakes you up in the middle of the night, there is a reason for it. In other words, He needs you to work with Him to facilitate some things in the Kingdom.

I would have missed out on so much had I not followed God's voice. So many messages, revelations, and songs would have been undiscovered. So many miracles and divine encounters may have never been received if I had not followed His leading and come into alignment with His will by yielding in prayer and fasting.

If God is waking you up in the middle of the night, stopping you through your day to pray, or encouraging you to call someone, those are Holy Spirit promptings, guiding you to His perfect will. Lives depend on you being alert and obedient to the voice of God.

Lives Depend on Your Obedience

One night, I was very tired and really wanted to go to bed. In my spirit, I heard that still small voice—a whisper with a sense of urgency: *"Philip, get on social media."*

I thought that was strange. Why would God want me to scroll down other people's pages? That almost seemed like it was not God. Yet peace accompanied that voice. My eyelids were closing. It was 1:00 in the morning, and I was so ready to go to sleep. Yet I heard clearly in my spirit, "Whatever you do, do not fall asleep."

As I scrolled through social media, I noticed that one of my leaders in the youth group had just deleted his page. This seemed very uncharacteristic of him because he was extremely active on social media. For this young man to delete his page was almost like he was deleting himself from life.

I immediately felt like I needed to go check on this leader. As I was getting dressed to go to his house, I received a text message from his close friend expressing concern: "Pastor, he is acting weird and saying strange things. I am worried about him."

That was a confirmation to what I had sensed. Within five minutes, I arrived at this young man's home and knocked on the door. When he opened it, I asked if everything was okay. He said he was fine, but I didn't believe him, so I asked him again.

My youth leader said, "I'm fine, but take these pills away from me so I don't overdose."

I was stunned. Had I not come, this young man most likely would have committed suicide. I spent the next two hours with him praying, crying—and, ultimately, laughing with him and encouraging him in the Lord. Finally, when I was assured that he was fine, I got in my car to go home.

On my way back home, all I could think about was, *What if I hadn't listened to God's voice to get on social media? What if I had gone to bed that night and fallen asleep instead of paying attention to the voice of the Holy Spirit?* I probably would have awakened to a phone call that I was going to conduct this young man's funeral!

I praised God the whole way home. I was so thankful for His intervention to save that young man's life. I was also thankful that His urgency kept me alert.

Being alert and sensitive to God's voice can literally stop tragedies, save lives, and cause the backslidden Christians to come alive to Christ again.

This all happened when I was regularly fasting off and on. I was deliberately training my flesh to be quiet while developing my spirit to hear and obey God's voice on a consistent basis. I most likely would have not heard His voice had I not been quieting down my flesh to be more sensitive to Him and to follow His direction.

Fasting is a mighty weapon that adds weight to our prayers, because each time we choose to humble ourselves before God, He gives us more grace (*see* James 4:6-7). Let's utilize every weapon available to us to render the enemy defenseless so we can defeat him on every side. Let's listen for the Holy Spirit's prompting, and then follow His way for us.

Living a fasted life will look different for each of us according to His specific direction to us. But humility, consecration, and hunger for God's Word and His presence are the common denominators of a lifestyle of intimacy and power with God.

STRONG AND COURAGEOUS

God has a plan for you. All you have to do is partner with Him and follow His voice. When you do that, you will *see* Him fight your battles. His plan for you is more than you can comprehend.

> *Look around [you, Habakkuk, replied the Lord]*
> *among the nations and see! And be astonished!*
> *Astounded! For I am putting into effect a work in*

your days [such] that you would not believe it if it were told you.

Habakkuk 1:5 AMPC

You will be astonished and astounded by how God comes through for you. He is doing something so great that if He were to show it to you, you would not believe it! The King of kings and Lord of Lords is working on your behalf. He needs you to strengthen yourself in prayer and the Word of God so that you are ready to move forward with what He has planned for you.

God's plans will be impossible for you to accomplish without Him. You might even think, *God, really? That is way over my head! How am I going to do that?* The simple answer is you aren't going to do it, but God will do it through you. It is your assignment, but His project!

When business executives travel all over the world on different assignments, the company they work for is responsible for paying their expenses incurred for the completion of that assignment. All of their travel, food, transportation, and living-arrangement expenses are paid for. The employee doesn't have to think about anything other than focusing on the completion of his or her assignment.

The same is true for us when we choose to accept a God-given assignment. God supplies what we need—in all areas. We just have to be strong and courageous as we fulfill our assignment.

Often during a fast, God will reveal assignments that you ignored. Fasting and praying heightens your spiritual senses while expanding your spiritual capacity so you can hear His voice and take hold of a neglected assignment once again with strength and courage.

Silencing your flesh to sensitize your spirit will make you more alert to hear God's voice and act on what He tells you. You will be more alert to make a course change. God will make it very clear to you if you are off track. And if you need to repent, God will direct you in making adjustments so your thoughts and actions get in agreement with His will and you can advance.

Sometimes repenting causes you to come out of your comfort zone. It takes courage to step out of your comfort zone and not look back.

Something I find fascinating about the eagle is when it leaves its nest, it never returns. God wants us to learn to fly! He wants us to leave our comfort zone and never come back.

There's no looking back with God—only forward! Even Jesus said, "Remember Lot's wife" (Luke 17:32) because she looked back and she became a pillar of salt. Never look back! Like the eagle, leave your comfort zone and learn to soar in the sky!

In fasting, God will challenge you to leave your comfort zone. He will challenge your faith. He will ask you, "Do you really want to know how to fly? Great! Go for it! Jump, and I will lead you." As you obey His prompting, you will be strong and courageous in accepting the assignment, and He will help you stay alert to hear His voice and direction on the path ahead. In the end, you will be astonished and astounded at all God has for you! Faith will rise in you to fulfill your assignment.

Do you sense that more in God is waiting for you? It's time for you to fast and pray as the mind of Christ is fully released in you to know His plan for your life. You will be astonished and astounded by the journey and path that He will show as you listen to His voice and give heed to His guidance.

SUPERNATURAL PROTECTION IS YOURS!

There was one year when I fasted almost continually. I became known as the fasting preacher. I had several long fasts throughout that year, and in between those long fasts, I fasted several times a week. It was in this intense season of fasting that my wife and I had the opportunity to travel to the United States to attend a conference we were very excited about. We lived in Moscow at the time, so we called my mother-in-law to ask if she could take care of our three-year-old daughter Mia for the time of our absence. She agreed, so Ella and I set off to the US.

About three or four days before our trip, all I could think about was the story of Job in the Bible. The thought that when he lost everything, he bowed down and worshiped God was astounding to me. I was meditating on this constantly. It just wouldn't let go of me. Job lost his wealth, his house, and even all his children, yet he would not curse God. Instead, at the revelation of his great loss, Job fell down and worshiped God.

Job stood up and tore his robe in grief. Then he shaved his head and fell to the ground to worship.

Job 1:20 NLT

We can only imagine how upset and disturbed Job was, yet he still worshiped God.

This story just wouldn't leave me. I got on the plane, and this story was in my head. I would board the next flight, and this story was in my head. Our travel time to the states from Moscow was 27 hours. That's six hours longer than what it usually takes to get to Tulsa, Oklahoma. And the entire time, this story was in my head.

I remember thinking, *Is the Holy Spirit trying to warn me about something? What is going on?*

All I could think about was Job falling down and worshiping. I would meditate on that one thought again and again. I knew I was hearing God's voice, but I was puzzled. I even wondered, *Is this the Holy Spirit telling me to pray against something? Is my Comforter trying to show me things to come?*

When the Spirit of truth comes, he will guide you into all truth. He will not speak on his own but will tell you what he has heard. He will tell you about the future.

John 16:13 NLT

I was aware and alert to all of this, but I had no fear. Throughout this time that I was meditating on these verses in Job, there was complete peace.

130

Peace I leave with you; my peace I give to you. Not as the world gives do I give to you. Let not your hearts be troubled, neither let them be afraid.

John 14:27 ESV

Finally, we landed in Tulsa where my Aunt Trula was meeting us to take us home from the airport. Exhausted and jet-lagged, we picked up our stuff at baggage claim and got in the car.

As we got on the highway, I knew I was about 15 minutes from bed, and I was ready for it. Suddenly we drove over something. I looked through the window and saw sparks flying out from underneath the car. I told my aunt, "We've got to stop! I'll get whatever we ran over from underneath the car, and we can go on."

At this time it was close to midnight and very dark, so I couldn't see anything. I reached my hands to grab whatever we ran over from underneath the car and realized I had a bed mattress in my hands. I couldn't believe my eyes. I really thought I was just tired and my brain was not functioning correctly, so I tried to pull it out again. Then reality hit me that someone had dropped a mattress on the highway, and it was stuck underneath our vehicle!

My Aunt Trula couldn't believe it! We all got out of the car and started walking away from it as she called a tow truck to pick up the car. We were all looking at each other in disbelief. This felt like a bad scene in a movie; it was so surreal and strange. We all walked about 50 feet away and waited for the tow truck to come.

Still not fully believing this was happening, I decided to check the car again. I circled the vehicle. In my spirit, I sensed that something very disturbing was about to happen. Then I saw the smoke. I knelt down to see where it was coming from and I realized that the mattress underneath the car was on fire. I thought it was about to blow. I ran to Ella and Aunt Trula and told them what I had seen. Aunt Trula shouted, "Run! There's a full tank of gas in the car!"

As the three of us ran, I looked behind just in time to watch the car burst into flames. It felt like a James Bond movie, only this was for real. As the car went up in flames, suddenly Ella and I remembered that our passports were in that car. Not only that, but she had also just renewed her green card, and my Russian visa was in the car as well.

We knew that without our passports, we wouldn't be going home to Russia until all of our lost documents had been renewed. That process was an expensive one that would take a lot of time. But besides all of this, we had left our daughter in Russia at her grandma's house. Our passports going up in flames meant that we would be stuck in the states and separated from our daughter for three or four months at least.

Besides that, my computer and iPad were also in that car. And our best clothes were in there. Everything that we had to wear for three weeks was in that car! We knew that potentially the only clothes we had for the trip were the clothes we had on.

This trip was supposed to be our vacation, but it had quickly turned into a nightmare scene. We had been excited about the conference we came to attend—then this happened.

As Ella clung to me, crying, I remembered what the Holy Spirit had been leading me to meditate on for the past week. When Job lost everything, he fell down and worshiped.

I looked at my wife and said, "If we lose everything today, we've lost nothing because we still have Jesus."

In the midst of total chaos, I had total peace.

YOU WILL PASS THROUGH THE FIRE

I prayed for God to stop the flames. The flames rose even higher!

I spoke to the sky, "Rain come—now!" At that moment, the back wheel blew up and flew 30 feet in my direction!

Things seemed to be getting worse, not better! I didn't know what was going on, but I had complete peace inside. I knew we would see a miracle.

As we watched the car turn into a mass of flames, smoke from the car rose hundreds of feet in the air. Finally, the fire department arrived. They immediately put out the fire, working swiftly and efficiently. Ella and I both believed there was hope that our passports somehow survived.

After they extinguished the fire and the smoke had cleared, I walked up to one of the firemen and asked, "Do you think our passports are still in there?"

The man looked at me strangely and replied, "No! If they were, then they are gone now!"

I replied, "Sir, my whole life was in that car, so I'm believing for a miracle."

"Okay, let's see," the fireman replied, kind of smirking as we walked toward what was left of the car.

As Ella and I approached the vehicle, we were absolutely shocked to see that it had literally burned to a crisp. As the fireman started removing rubble to look for any surviving possessions, he found what looked like a purse. Ella shouted, "My purse!" The purse itself was destroyed, but to our amazement, there were items inside that seemed untouched by the flames.

Inside Ella's purse was a wallet specifically for travel. Inside that wallet was a plastic envelope. And inside that envelope were our passports—a little scorched, but intact and usable for travel.

Ella and I started shouting and praising the Lord! The fireman said he had never seen anything like it before. The next thing that he pulled out of the car was my wife's Bible. It was in the fire, but it did not burn! I thought about the bush that was on fire in the Old Testament but wasn't consumed by the fire (*see* Exod. 3:2). I also thought of Daniel's three friends in the fiery furnace, who emerged without even the smell of smoke on them (*see* Dan. 3:25-27)! I was so amazed by the situation. It was a miracle!

Our passports were completely intact, and the Bible did not burn. This Bible we still see every day as we walk in our home. It lies in plain sight for all to see as a constant reminder of God's faithfulness.

As Ella and I continued to search through the items, we found my laptop computer, burned to a crisp. Hundreds of messages and notes were in that computer. Unfinished songs and even a book I was working on were in that computer. My mind told me, *You have lost it all.* But then a sense of peace rose within me. I thought, *Look what God has already done. All is well.*

Then I heard God speak to my heart, "Just trust Me!" I knew He would take care of us.

We also found my iPad that I had filled with notes and used when I preached. It didn't work because water had gotten under the screen as a result of the firemen putting out the fire. We also found a shirt or two that we could wear the next day. All our clothes and shoes were destroyed, but we were so happy about our passports and the Bible that didn't burn that we really didn't care about what we would wear the next day.

As we were rejoicing, a team from a local news station arrived on the scene. No one had called them; they just showed up. I guess they thought a burning car and a family stranded on the side of the road could make for a great story. But they were surprised to find a family rejoicing and praising God when it had seemed that they had lost everything.

The news reporter immediately started to interview me. I figured that if I preached, they wouldn't show it on television, so I decided to preach boldly to the cameraman. I said things like, "It's amazing how God put His hand on these passports to protect them. It's a miracle. Jesus is Lord!"

By about 3 a.m., we were sleeping in our beds. Everything that had happened seemed like a dream. It seemed so unreal, yet it was reality. The next morning, my Aunt Trula woke me up by sticking her iPad in my face and saying, "Philip, you have to watch this!"

To my complete surprise, it was the 6 a.m. news, and there I was saying, "It's amazing how God put His hand on our passports to protect them. It's a miracle!" I was shocked. They actually aired me praising God about our testimony! Within the next half hour, our phone rang. It was the news station again. They wanted to come and get another interview with me. Shocked by it all, I was ecstatic to be able to share my faith on local news in Tulsa, Oklahoma.

The news station showed that second interview on the 6 p.m. news that evening. I was shocked by it all, but I still had no clothes for Ella and me. Furthermore, my iPad and computer were not working.

We also needed to call our insurance company so we could get reimbursed for the car and everything else that was lost. We knew that insurance companies generally will try to not recompense losses, but we were sure that just as God had already done great things, He would continue to provide.

Ella and I agreed that all our electronics would be reimbursed, along with all our clothing. The insurance company quickly replied to notify us that the car and all electronics would be compensated, but none of our personal items would be compensated. Although this did not make us happy, it did not steal our joy. God had been so good to us, we knew He had more miracles in store for us!

As I walked into the computer store to get my new computer, I was excited but nervous about the possibility of losing all my information in the transfer. We purchased the new computer and I set my old computer on the table to see if the transfer of information would be successful.

When the technician saw my computer he said, "What happened, bro?"

I replied, "Dude, my computer seriously overheated."

He laughed, and then I told him the story. He was shocked! I was so blessed to be able to share my testimony everywhere I went!

The technician told me there was a very slim chance that I would be able to get any information off that hard drive since it was so badly burned. I laughed and said that I thought it would be all right. After all the Lord had done, I was trusting Him to care for every detail.

When I returned for my laptop in a couple of hours, the technician was shocked. I lost absolutely nothing! In fact, the transfer went so well that the same documents that were open on my previous computer were open on my new one— another miracle! I went home so blessed and ecstatic over the goodness of God!

Still, my iPad with so many messages was damaged. I used it constantly when I preached. I continued to believe that somehow it would work. I did not throw it away but put it in the car trunk instead. A few days later I decided to throw it away. But to my surprise, the water under the screen had evaporated. I plugged it into the charger—and it worked! I had lost nothing! All my family pictures were there, and all my messages were intact. Another miracle!

Later I figured out what had happened. All this occurred in the summer. The temperature outside in Tulsa was more than 100 degrees all week, so the temperature in the trunk was even hotter, which caused the water to evaporate out from the screen. The strange thing was there were three little spots that looked like holes but they weren't. At first, I thought I had holes in my iPad but then I realized they were just spots—left to remind me that God had saved my iPad.

HE COMES TO OUR AID

You might be wondering why I'm sharing all these stories. First of all, I want to praise God for all the little details, not just the big things. But secondly, I was greatly encouraged that the Lord had impressed upon me to pray with fasting more than usual before this incident happened. He was not only engaging my faith, but He was also stirring me to pray ahead for what was to come.

As I mentioned earlier, praying in the Spirit covers far more than we realize. It is multi-dimensional. Romans 8:26 (AMPC) states:

> *So too the [Holy] Spirit comes to our aid and bears us up in our weakness; for we do not know what prayer to offer nor how to offer it worthily as we ought, but the Spirit Himself goes to meet our supplication and pleads in our behalf with unspeakable yearnings and groanings too deep for utterance.*

At any point in that situation, beginning when we ran over the mattress in the road and sparks began to fly, we could have been killed. But the Lord protected us. Not only did He keep us safe, His Spirit showed me how to respond from the book of Job. We worshiped God when it seemed as though we had lost everything. But that worship and gratefulness kept His power flowing on our behalf until every vital thing was restored.

That accident certainly wasn't the will of God; it was a work of the devil that came to steal, kill, and to destroy. But God went before us to prepare the way, and His presence gave us peace in the midst of it all.

I can't encourage you enough: Whenever you sense the Lord drawing you into extended times of prayer and reading His Word or to fast one or several meals, please follow the Lord in it. He knows what's necessary to prepare you for what is to come!

I was so shocked through the whole ordeal that I forgot about one very important thing: I brought my shofar from Russia to play in churches when I led worship. In the midst of everything, I had forgotten it was in the car. That shofar was very important to me, so I went to the junkyard where our car had been towed. I looked inside to see if I could find my shofar. Sure enough, it was there. The only problem was it had turned from a beautiful brown and beige to charcoal black because it was burned. It wasn't destroyed, just severely darkened from the flames. But the strange thing was that the sound of it had changed.

The tuning of my shofar was in the key of A when I got it. That key sounds very "victorious," but it was not the tone I wanted. When choosing my shofar, I blew at least 20 others searching for a sound that would match one of my favorite chords—F sharp minor (F#m). Unfortunately, I didn't find it, but I did find one that was in the key of A, so I was somewhat pleased. I asked the men selling me the shofar what they thought. They said this was a good one and that a shofar in F#m didn't exist.

As I looked at my shofar after it had been burned in the car, part of me wanted to throw it away because it was an ugly, charcoal black and wasn't beautiful anymore. But something in me said to check the tuning before I threw it away.

I immediately contacted a friend who played piano so I could check the tuning of my shofar. I was completely shocked when I discovered that the tune of my burned shofar was now F#m—the exact key I wanted but had been unable to find! God had tuned the key of my shofar down one and half steps to give me the desire of my heart! I was astounded—another miracle!

No one knew about my desired tuning for that shofar. But God knew—just like He knows the secret desires of your heart. God took a tragedy and turned it into a blessing even to the tiniest details. He will do the same with you!

Since then, I have used this shofar hundreds of times in worship and have seen God powerfully touch so many hearts as it is played. I am blessed as well because of the powerful story behind it!

All of this was amazing, but with God, things only get better. Before I had come to the states, I had contacted different churches and ministries stating that I would be honored to serve and tell my story as a missionary from Russia. As a youth pastor, I was hoping to speak to youth and inspire them to serve God with all their hearts. Sadly,

I received zero response. It seemed like no one wanted to hear my story. But when people turned on the news and saw my testimony, they suddenly wanted me to share my story in their church.

So as a result of the accident, I was able to share my testimony not only on the news, but in several churches! I got to tell them about all the miracles—the car, passports, Bible, computer, iPad, and shofar, as well as the unexpected invitations to other churches. Through this entire situation, people donated money to me and Ella so we could buy new clothes—which turned out to be better than our clothes that burned in the fire!

The only thing I had asked God to answer that I hadn't seen come to pass was for insurance to cover the cost of the clothes we had lost. My wife and I had written out what was the approximate cost of the lost clothes and submitted that amount to the insurance company. Their response was, "We will compensate you for all electronics, but lost clothing is your responsibility." This answer didn't bless me and Ella, but we were so grateful for everything that had been restored and compensated for that we decided we wouldn't worry about it. Besides, God had taken care of everything else, so we knew that He would be able to take care of this as well.

Soon our time in America came to an end, and we returned to Moscow. Three months after all this happened, we received a phone call from the insurance company asking our forgiveness for not immediately compensating us for all our clothing. This was a true miracle! Insurance companies generally do not call you to ask for forgiveness for not immediately compensating your losses! We saw the favor of the Lord demonstrated before our very eyes. Although fire literally had tried to consume us, the favor of God surrounded us like a shield (*see* Ps. 5:12).

I believe all of this happened not by accident but because of the intense season of fasting I had offered to the Lord as worship prior to this trip.

Just as Job bowed in worship when he lost everything, my wife and I worshiped the Lord as we stood on the brink of losing everything. I believe it was at that very moment when our miracle took place.

In that moment of intense pressure, I would not have automatically entered into prayer and worship, regardless of what I saw and felt, if I had not been training my flesh to spend time in God's presence through extended prayer, fasting, and study of the Word.

Choosing to train and discipline the flesh with godly practices produces strength that will rise in our spirits to fortify us when we need it most.

Prayer and fasting made room for God to be exalted in my life, in my schedule, in my thoughts. God will honor those who honor Him. I esteemed His Word and His presence in my life above my desire for food or other activities, and He magnified His strength on our behalf to fulfill the promises of His Word and to manifest His power, His favor, and His presence in all the ways we needed Him.

You can trust Him to do the same for you.

When you walk through the fire, you shall not be burned, nor shall the flame scorch you.

Isaiah 43:2 NKJV

MY PRAYER

Father, thank You for teaching me sensitivity through fasting and praying. I know that as I seek You, You will make me alert, strong, and courageous. I will be successful in fulfilling all You have planned for me to do. I know that as I fast, I hear Your voice clearly because all other voices are drowned out. I promise if I hear Your voice in the middle of the night or day, I will be alert and spend time with You. I know that as I do this, I will grow in knowing You and lives will literally be saved through prayer. As I follow Your voice, I know I will come into alignment with Your perfect will for my life and will see Your favor surround me like a shield. Thank You for teaching me, Heavenly Father. In the name of Jesus I pray. Amen.

CHAPTER 7

SPIRITUAL BENEFITS OF FASTING AND PRAYER: SETTING THE CAPTIVES FREE

THE COMBINATION OF fasting with prayer propels your worship and prayer into a multi-dimensional function in the Spirit. It takes on an added measure of weight in the Spirit because of the humility and spiritual hunger that anchors your fast.

As we have already considered in Matthew 6, the foundation of fasting is humility. Jesus spoke extensively on this subject.

Many blessings and revelations unfold in your life when you are in a place of humility. When you show God that you care more about spending time with Him than you care about your next meal, God views that fast as a powerful act of consecration that will produce great results by causing His own heart to be released in situations.

1. FASTING SETS THE CAPTIVES FREE

This is the kind of fasting I want... Let the oppressed
go free, and remove the chains that bind people.

Isaiah 58:6 NLT

Isaiah 58:6-11 describes the motivation and the results of fasting that God desires. He wants the captives to be free.

When I was a youth pastor, there was a certain young man from my congregation who was walking away from the things of God. I attempted to reach out to him, but he would not get back to me. I called him relentlessly, but he never picked up the phone. I tried messaging him on multiple platforms of social media. Nothing was working. He was ignoring all my calls. I knew that the only way that I would bring him in was by praying. During this time, I was also in an extended fast before the Lord.

That day I realized that I could not reach this young man naturally. I understood the only way I was going to reach him was in the Spirit. That day I focused on him in prayer. I cried out for him to awaken to God's voice. During that prayer of intercession, I felt something shift in the Spirit. I knew that God had gotten hold of his heart. Almost immediately I felt the burden of prayer lift.

Many people have told me to put a time limit on prayer. I don't agree. You must pray until you feel the breakthrough. Persevere in prayer until the burden of prayer lifts.

I felt a sense of peace on me. It was the peace that passes all natural understanding and logic, according to Philippians 4:7.

In the natural, I didn't see anything happening, but I knew that prayer had made power available and that this brother had been realigned to God's perfect will.

You see, in the natural my logic was telling me, "You will never get hold of him. He is gone." But in the Spirit, I felt like I had already gotten the breakthrough. That peace was stronger than what I was seeing in the natural. In that moment, I knew that this brother would contact me, so I calmed down and stopped trying to contact him.

The next day I got a call. "Philip, I have to meet with you." It was the young man I had been praying for.

I replied that I didn't have time in the day, which was true. I did, however, have time later that evening. But I told the young man that he would have to come to where I was; otherwise, I would not be able to meet with him. He replied, "I will do anything you ask. I just have to meet you today!"

Suddenly this brother had changed from being disconnected and disinterested to desiring to be reconnected and restored. I knew it was a direct result of interceding for him while I was fasting.

That night we met. The young man traveled at least an hour or more to get to my location. It was not convenient for him, but he genuinely didn't care. He just wanted to see me. When we finally met, he asked for my forgiveness. I counseled him, and we took Communion together. That evening he went from being backslidden to on fire for God. I knew when he left my apartment in Moscow that day—God had intervened.

He didn't come to see me because of any irresistible persuasiveness on my part. No, he was set free because of the power of fasting and praying. One powerful hour of intercession for him brought him back to the Kingdom, and he became one of the strongest leaders in the youth ministry.

That was the day when I understood as never before that fasting and praying causes the captives to be set free. Only later did I find this truth in Isaiah 58 as I was reading a book that changed my life—*The Hidden Power of Fasting and Praying* by Mahesh Chavda. It was in this book that I was reminded that fasting sets the captives free.

I have shared this story and other experiences not to brag about my walk with the Lord, but to brag about Him and His power that is available to all of us. God has given us a powerful weapon to defeat the enemy. Using this weapon equips us to set the captives free.

It doesn't matter how far your friends and relatives may have wandered away from the Lord—God can get them back. Prisoners of the world who still have hope must be brought into the Kingdom of light. Your prayer and fasting will release an anointing upon them to destroy every chain and translate them from the kingdom of darkness into the Kingdom of light by God's power!

Not only will the prisoners come home, but they will also get double for their trouble.

> *Come back to the place of safety, all you prisoners who still have hope! I promise this very day that I will repay two blessings for each of your troubles.*
> Zechariah 9:12 NLT

Instead of shame and dishonor, you will enjoy a double share of honor. You will possess a double portion of prosperity in your land, and everlasting joy will be yours.

Isaiah 61:7 NLT

When you humble yourself to seek the Lord through prayer and fasting, He will not only encourage you with His presence, but He will also manifest His goodness to bring restoration to your life and to others.

RECOVER EVERY SINGLE THING!

When we lived in Tulsa, our pastor, Paul Brady, was preaching from 1 Samuel 30, and he said something powerful that inspired me greatly. When David and his men returned home to Ziklag, they discovered that their enemies had not only burned and plundered the town, but they had also carried off the men's wives and children. In the trauma of that moment, with his despairing men threatening to stone him, David encouraged himself in the Lord and then inquired of Him whether he should pursue the enemy and overtake them. The Lord told David to pursue and overtake, for he would surely recover every single thing (*see* 1 Sam. 30:8).

Pastor Paul said, "That's what the Lord accomplishes in our lives. He brings rest through restoration." Then he gave us the acronym that the Lord had shown him: R.E.S.T.—"Recover Every Single Thing."

Those four words resonated so strongly in my heart. God is in the business of recovering every single thing. Not only will prisoners come home, but your relatives and friends will come back to the house of God. Furthermore, they will get double for their trouble!

Fasting and praying positions you to cooperate with God to expedite this process of recovering every single thing as you yield to selfless intercession for captives to be released from bondage and come home to God.

2. FASTING AND PRAYING UNLOCK GREAT COMPASSION

> *Share your food with the hungry, and give shelter to the homeless. Give clothes to those who need them, and do not hide from relatives who need your help.*
>
> Isaiah 58:7 NLT

When your fasting and your praying are rooted in humility, the fruit of compassion will grow. Your heart will give large expression to the Father's heart because of your own selfless surrender to Him in fasting and in prayer.

Situations that you used to be able to ignore, you cannot ignore any longer. It causes you to not walk by people who are in need without an awareness of their bondage and pain. Fasting and praying causes your heart to become more like the Heavenly Father's. It causes you to become like the Good Samaritan who stopped to help the man lying on the ground, robbed and beaten by robbers. It causes you to clothe and feed those who are in need. This kind of compassion moves you.

COMPASSION

Fasting causes compassion to rise inside of you. Jesus is a prime example of this compassion. If Jesus was led by the Spirit of God into the wilderness to fast and to pray before His earthly ministry began, how much more do you and I need to fast? I believe that because Jesus fasted, He increased His compassion for humanity. Through fasting Jesus connected to the Heavenly Father's heart, and because of that He was able to connect to the people's hearts and minister to them.

MOVED WITH COMPASSION

Let's take a look at how Jesus mirrored the heart of the Father.

> *But when he saw the multitudes, he was moved with compassion on them, because they fainted, and were scattered abroad, as sheep having no shepherd.*
>
> Matthew 9:36 KJV

Matthew 9:36 says that Jesus was moved with compassion. Compassion is mentioned 41 times in the King James Version. I would say that having a heart full of compassion is a big thing that must be cultivated in the heart of every believer—and certainly in the heart of every worship leader, volunteer, and minister of the Gospel.

As ministers of the Gospel, we can't just be anointed in speaking or leading worship and yet forget to have compassion for the world, or even our own lost family members. We can get so consumed with serving the Body that we forget about the world that needs salvation. Jesus did not fall into this lie because He was constantly spending time with His Father in prayer. The more He prayed, the more the nature and the love of Father were revealed through Him.

A great scripture that portrays the heart of the Father is Isaiah 1:17 (NLT):

> *Learn to do good. Seek justice. Help the oppressed. Defend the cause of orphans. Fight for the rights of widows.*

This is what Jesus did through His ministry! The reason He did this is that this heart of compassion was cultivated through a life of prayer with His Heavenly Father!

Here are several passages that explain how Jesus was dependent on prayer. Many of these scriptures took place after a strenuous day of ministry. Instead of sleeping after ministering to multiple thousands of people, Jesus went to pray. In the early hours of the morning before ministry, Jesus was praying.

The following are several examples that reveal how Jesus went to ministry in prayer and from ministry to prayer.

> *After He had sent the crowds away, He went up on the mountain by Himself to pray; and when it was evening, He was there alone.*
> Matthew 14:23 NASB

> *And He went a little beyond them, and fell on His face and prayed, saying, "My Father, if it is*

possible, let this cup pass from Me; yet not as I will, but as You will."

Matthew 26:39 NASB

He went away again a second time and prayed, saying, "My Father, if this cannot pass away unless I drink it, Your will be done."

Matthew 26:42 NASB

And He left them again, and went away and prayed a third time, saying the same thing once more.

Matthew 26:44 NASB

In the early morning, while it was still dark, Jesus got up, left the house, and went away to a secluded place, and was praying there.

Mark 1:35 NASB

After bidding them farewell, He left for the mountain to pray.

Mark 6:46 NASB

They came to a place named Gethsemane; and He said to His disciples, "Sit here until I have prayed."

Mark 14:32 NASB

And He went a little beyond them, and fell to the ground and began to pray that if it were possible, the hour might pass Him by.

Mark 14:35 NASB

Again He went away and prayed, saying the same words.

Mark 14:39 NASB

But Jesus Himself would often slip away to the wilderness and pray.

Luke 5:16 NASB

It was at this time that He went off to the mountain to pray, and He spent the whole night in prayer to God.

Luke 6:12 NASB

Jesus started each day with prayer and ended it with prayer. *His dependency was not His physical strength or financial support of the ministry. Rather, it was in the strength that He received through intimacy with God.* It was in that place that Jesus' compassion for the world grew. It was cultivated by the Spirit. It was cultivated by the heart of the Father!

Here are several scriptures about compassion in the gospels.

And Jesus called His disciples to Him, and said, "I feel compassion for the people, because they have remained with Me now three days and have nothing to eat; and I do not want to send them away hungry, for they might faint on the way."

Matthew 15:32 NASB

When He went ashore, He saw a large crowd, and felt compassion for them and healed their sick.

Matthew 14:14 NASB

Moved with compassion, Jesus touched their eyes; and immediately they regained their sight and followed Him.

Matthew 20:34 NASB

When Jesus went ashore, He saw a large crowd, and He felt compassion for them because they were like sheep without a shepherd; and He began to teach them many things.

Mark 6:34 NASB

When the Lord saw her, He felt compassion for her, and said to her, "Do not weep."

Luke 7:13 NASB

The more time Jesus spent with the Father, the more the heart of the Father was developed in Him. The Father's heart is a heart full of compassion for the world.

I want to look at the second phrase from Matthew 9:36 we have been talking about. Jesus was "moved with compassion." For years I read that and wondered, *What does that mean?* Then finally I decided to study it out.

In Thayer's Greek Lexicon, I found that the phrase "moved with compassion" (transliteration: *splagchnizomai*) meant "to be moved with compassion, have compassion (for the bowels were thought to be the seat of love and pity)."

The best explanation I've heard on the usage of that word is given by my father, Rick Renner—a well-known Bible teacher whose expertise in New Testament Greek reveals hidden meaning in Scripture.

In the July 30 passage of his book *Sparkling Gems 2*, Dad writes:

I want to focus on the phrase "bowels of mercies," which sounds very strange in today's vernacular but conveys a powerful message. It is a translation of two Greek words, *splagnon* and *oiktirmos*. The word *splagnon* refers to *the inner organs of a human body*, or more specifically, *the bowels*, and the word *oiktirmos* denotes *compassion* or *a deeply felt urge to help relieve some kind of pain or sorrow*.

Before I elaborate further on the Greek word *splagnon* ("bowels"), I must ask you to pardon me in advance for being so blunt with my explanation. However, it is important to consider the function of bowels in order to understand the reason why that word is used in connection with "mercy" and "compassion" in the New Testament.

Physically, when your bowels move, you feel it *deeply*. When the process is done, the bowels have made *a physical deposit* and rid the body of human waste. The purpose of these feelings, however, is not superficial—they are a sign that the intestines are working to push waste through the system and out of the body.

Thus, by using the word *splagnon*, Paul was saying that *deep feelings of compassion* should do more than merely provoke pity for a person's situation; they should spur you to action. When these feelings begin to well up deep within your spirit, you must surrender to them and let them work through your inner man until they manifest through your words and actions. As you do this, God's Spirit simultaneously works through you to reach out and make a spiritual deposit.

When I explained this to my daughter Mia, who was nine at the time, she was very intrigued. So I asked her if she understood why this word was used in the Bible.

She replied, "I get it! There was something on the inside of Jesus that caused Him to take action. He could not stay still. Love caused him to move! That's really cool, Daddy!"

I told her that she'd done well and explained to her that the love of God on the inside of us causes us to do the same. Because of compassion moving inside us, as Christians we will not be able to ignore someone who needs to be healed. We cannot ignore a starving, homeless person. The love of God within compels us to take action.

This is the same compassion that moved Jesus. And He said that the things He did we will also do and more so if we are spending time with the Father every day.

The second part of verse 36 describes the spiritual state the world is in: "They fainted, and were scattered abroad, as sheep having no shepherd."

Fainted: The John Gill's Exposition of the Bible describes this word as "tired and fatigued; sickness; pain; a people distressed and with no answers; tortured from going from place to place with no purpose."

Scattered: I have read multiple commentaries on this subject, and all of them support the idea that this word pertains to the spiritual state of the people. They were scattered in their minds and scattered by the religious sects in Greco-Roman period. This would make perfect sense, considering that all the arguments Jesus had with the Pharisees in the gospels were of a religious nature. Multiple times in

Scripture, Jesus was judged for healing on the Sabbath. Whenever Jewish tradition was at odds with the loving compassion of the Father, Jesus followed the direction of the Holy Spirit. He saw that the people were scattered and fainted. Again, compassion moved Jesus to take action.

The religious leaders who challenged Jesus were full of the traditions of men, but there was no life-giving power in their lives. They followed regulations, yet saw no change in their lives. This is an accurate picture of religion in the Church today. There are millions of believers who go to church, yet live with no power.

Jesus is still seeing many who are fainted and scattered. His compassion moves Him to align the Church and pour out His Spirit. If we have ears to hear, we will hear and change!

SHEEP HAVING NO SHEPHERD

Two things are important to understand about sheep:

1. Sheep depend completely on the habitat and environment they are being brought up in. If the environment is dirty, the sheep will not do well. If the environment is well taken care of, sheep will thrive.

2. Sheep are followers. They will follow the leader anywhere. Sheep choose a leader in the flock. Many times without a shepherd, they will follow the leader in the flock. Sheep will follow a leader; it doesn't matter whether

that leader is good or bad, smart or stupid—
they just follow.

In 2006, in eastern Turkey four hundred sheep all followed the lead sheep into a 15-meter or 50-foot ravine—and they all died. You can see from this example that sheep desperately need a shepherd. Sheep that follow other sheep are vulnerable and at risk. Sheep are lost without a shepherd!

It's amazing to me that Jesus used this example to describe the multitudes that followed. He said they were like sheep without a shepherd. In doing this, Jesus fulfilled prophecy spoken hundreds of years earlier:

> *As a shepherd looks after his scattered flock when he is with them, so will I look after my sheep. I will rescue them from all the places where they were scattered on a day of clouds and darkness.*
>
> Ezekiel 34:12

This again pertains to the spiritual state of the multitudes. Their leaders kept them bound beneath the weight of powerless traditions. As a result, the lives of the people were powerless, which left them vulnerable and at risk with no real understanding of the God they were trying to serve.

Jesus called the leaders who kept the people in that state hypocrites, vipers, and polished tombs on the outside but with everything dead on the inside. Religious leaders were causing the people to grow faint and be scattered like a sheep with no shepherd. They were like the sheep who led the 400 others into a ravine that killed them all. Jesus spoke to these leaders harshly because of His great love for people. These leaders who studied the Scriptures should have known and understood, but instead they were blind to the truth while claiming to see, and they caused the people to also be blind.

Jesus fiercely went out to rescue those who were fainting, scattered, like sheep without a shepherd. He was moved with compassion. He felt the people's pain and therefore took action by fighting for them against the religious leaders and healing them of all of their diseases. Jesus spoke up for those who couldn't speak up for themselves. In doing this, He fulfilled Proverbs 31:8: "Speak up for those who cannot speak for themselves, for the rights of all who are destitute."

You might ask yourself, *Why is this in a book on fasting?* Because these matters deal with our heart motives, and that is the power of fasting. When we humble ourselves before God to seek Him in fasting and prayer, we surrender our hearts to be transformed and conformed to God's heart. Fasting engages our relationship with God. It is not to be a religious exercise.

We will minister and pray differently if we understand the Father's heart for people and genuinely care about the state of the flock we are leading. We will preach, usher, and volunteer differently if we understand that people are scattered, fainting, and like a sheep without a shepherd.

The tactics that the enemy used in the gospels are the same tactics he uses today. When you are serving in church in any capacity, you are not doing anyone a favor; you are not performing a job. Service in the church is a privilege and a calling to represent God's heart to people who need to know Him and experience His love and power in their lives.

Your service is to be a calling fulfilled with a heart of compassion, cultivated by time spent with the Heavenly Father just as Jesus did. Time spent with the Lord in fasting and prayer fashions you into a laborer of great effectiveness for the Lord's harvest.

> *Then saith he unto his disciples, The harvest truly is plenteous, but the labourers are few; pray ye therefore the Lord of the harvest, that he will send forth labourers into his harvest.*
>
> Matthew 9:37-38 KJV

I am writing this book because I believe that you are a laborer. I believe that as you are reading this book, the fire of God is burning inside of you. The Holy Spirit right now is activating the compassion of God on the inside of you, and that compassion will cause you to take action. As you spend time with the Father, you are energized and filled with God's Spirit. The Holy Spirit is convicting and realigning things on the inside of you right now. You are a laborer, and you will go out and harvest the field. You will go after those who have been scattered or who have fainted, like sheep without any shepherd other than the religious system!

My Prayer

> *Father, I thank You for teaching me every day. I thank You that as I fast, You are expanding my capacity to receive You. As I fast and spend time in Your presence, my heart becomes more like Yours.*

As I spend time with You, I can feel compassion rise within me. Just like You, Lord, I make a decision to love the scattered, the faint, and those who have no shepherd. I know that as I fast, You will show me how to love those who have been lied to by religion—those who have so much knowledge of God, yet do not know You and are completely void of Your power. As I fast and pray, You give me wisdom on how to reach those who seem unreachable. You give me wisdom and power to set the captives free.

You are the King of kings and Lord of Lords, Jesus, and I commit my life to You. You are my everything!

Thank You for teaching me how to fast and pray, Heavenly Father, in the name of Jesus I pray. Amen.

CHAPTER 8

HARVEST TIME

THE WORLD MUST come to Jesus. I can almost hear you saying, "Philip, why are you talking about evangelism in a book about fasting?" Well, if you are a believer who fasts on a regular basis, a desire will grow in you to talk about Him. As a result of fasting and praying, you will overflow with God and you will not be able to hold it in. That is the purpose of a fasted life—to present your life as a vessel God can fill to over-flowing with Himself for the benefit of others.

Let's consider what Jesus told His disciples when He gave them what we call the Great Commission:

> And then he told them, "Go into all the world and preach the Good News to everyone. Anyone who believes and is baptized will be saved. But anyone who refuses to believe will be condemned. These miraculous signs will accompany those who believe: They will cast out demons in my name, and they will speak in new languages. They will be able to handle snakes with safety, and if they drink anything poisonous, it won't hurt them.

*They will be able to place their hands on the sick,
and they will be healed."*

Mark 16:15-18 NLT

These are the last words Jesus spoke before He ascended from the earth. He saved the best for last!

In this passage, Jesus is talking about the authority we carry to heal the sick, cast out demons, raise the dead, and pick up any deadly thing, rendering it incapable of producing harm. These are the signs that will follow those who believe.

Do you believe these signs will follow you? Fasting and praying will draw you into a position of such communion with God that faith in His Word and compassion for the world will increase inside you, compelling you to reach out to fulfill the Great Commission.

EQUIPPED FOR EFFECTIVE SERVICE

You can take deliberate steps to become a valuable instrument for the harvest. As you increase your consecration to walk with the Lord through fasting and prayer, you will experience a cleansing of your character by conforming your thoughts and behavior to His Word. Through this process of cleansing your character, you'll find that the fruit of the Spirit, the gifts of the Spirit, and Spirit-empowered evangelism will begin to operate or will increase in your life. The gifts of the Spirit are not just for the Church—they are mainly for evangelism in the world!

The fruits of the Spirit are fundamental in this process of spiritual growth because they enable your life to showcase the ways of God as you demonstrate the works of God through the gifts of the Spirit. Galatians 5:22-24 (KJV) states:

> *But the fruit of the Spirit is love, joy, peace, long-suffering, gentleness, goodness, faith, meekness, temperance: against such there is no law. And they that are Christ's have crucified the flesh with the affections and lusts.*

The "fruits" of the recreated spirit are the character traits of Christ. As Christians, we are to be gleaming with Christ's character, reflecting Him in all our ways and responses. Kind, loving, disciplined, hardworking, and faithful—these are just a few of the qualities that should be evident in our lives as we manifest Christ's glory, not only through our words but also through our actions. We're not to just talk the walk; we must walk the walk.

The gifts of the Spirit have a distinct function and they should be a part of every Christian's arsenal. First Corinthians 12:4-11 (KJV) cites them:

> *Now there are diversities of gifts, but the same Spirit. And there are differences of administrations, but the same Lord. And there are diversities of operations, but it is the same God which worketh all in all. But the manifestation of the Spirit is given to every man to profit withal. For to one is given by the Spirit the word of wisdom; to another the word of knowledge by the same Spirit; to another faith by the same Spirit; to another the gifts of healing by the same Spirit; to another the working of miracles; to another prophecy; to*

another discerning of spirits; to another divers kinds of tongues; to another the interpretation of tongues: but all these worketh that one and the selfsame Spirit, dividing to every man severally as he will.

These gifts are not only for the benefit of the Church but also to reach and reveal God's goodness to the world.

I remember waking up one morning with a strong sense of expectation that God was going to use me that day. I went to the airport, and the Lord told to me to bubble-wrap my bag before I got on the plane. This is common practice overseas so that no one steals your belongings, but I had never done it. But in that moment, God was telling me to do something I did not want to do and that would cost money. I knew it was not for protection because I had total peace about my stuff, so it didn't make any sense. God must have wanted me to do it for some other reason.

Reluctantly I went up to the station to wrap my bag. As soon as I saw the young man performing this service, I knew why God told me to wrap my bag. It was time for me to act on what the Holy Spirit wanted. The amount of inconvenience and money it cost me didn't matter compared to the value of making an eternal impact on this individual's life.

I walked up to this young man and knew supernaturally by the word of knowledge that I was to pray for his mother who was dealing with cancer. I asked him, "Can I pray for your mother?" Immediately he was in tears. In that moment he gave his life to the Lord, right there in the airport.

It made my day to see God step into that young man's life to bring salvation and healing. That was the day God revealed to me that the gifts of the Spirit are key tools for evangelism in the world, not just vehicles of His power in church services.

Holy Spirit will help and direct you in this area. Spirit-led evangelism will flow almost effortlessly through a fasted life, because when you consecrate yourself to please God's heart you will quickly discover that people are on His heart.

That morning at the airport, I was tired and wasn't thinking about ministry. But I woke up that morning with an expectation for God to use me. What was the result of that expectation? The glory of God that was burning inside me poured through me to manifest and bless someone else. God is so good!

Giving a word of knowledge resulted in the expansion of the Kingdom of God when I ministered to that young man in the airport. The Bible instructs us to desire or to hunger for spiritual gifts (*see* 1 Cor. 14:1). When we do this, they will operate in our daily lives as the Spirit of God leads us. The gifts will also be activated in worship and ministry.

This works for every believer—no exceptions—and that includes you. You can manifest the glory of God wherever you go in every arena of life. If you are truly drawing upon God's Word and His presence every day through a lifestyle of intimate communion, then what He pours into you will flow out through you to others. If you have a lifestyle of prayer, it will manifest itself as compassion for the world.

Make a decision today not just to go to church and receive the glory. Decide that you will take that same presence to the world and release the glory of God into people's lives so they can be changed!

The Bible clearly says it's more blessed to give than to receive (*see* Acts 20:35). You are a carrier of the glory. The same power that resurrected Christ from the dead is inside of you (*see* Rom. 8:11)! So go manifest the power of God! Go give the world the glory that is on the inside of you. God is with you, and His compassion will move you to manifest Him every single day of your life. Go for it! God is with you.

A fasted lifestyle will increase your sensitivity to the Spirit of God to live like this. As a result, your life will align with God's desires. This kind of lifestyle will produce the results of God's chosen fast—compassion that brings salvation, deliverance, and healing to yourself and others.

> *Is this not the fast that I have chosen: to loose the bands of wickedness, to undo the heavy burdens, to let the oppressed go free, and that you break every yoke? Is it not to share your bread with the hungry, and that you bring to your house the poor who are cast out; when you see the naked, that you cover him, and not hide yourself from your own flesh?*
>
> Isaiah 58:6-7 NKJV

> *Then your salvation will come like the dawn, and your wounds will quickly heal.*
>
> Isaiah 58:8 NLT

When you fast and pray, God will align you with His perfect will. However, this is only possible if you hear *and* obey. If you fast and hear God's voice, but you don't obey what He has told you, you have only fulfilled a religious obligation that has no power. You must hear His voice and obey. When you do that, God can change things inside you. Obedience will bring your heart and mindset into agreement with His.

Let me give you an example from my own life. The first time I fasted and prayed for 40 days, I continually asked God, "Lord, use me. I want You to use me in a mighty way!" I must have prayed that prayer almost every day.

One day as I was praying that, I heard God say, "Philip, you want Me to use you, right?"

I quickly replied, "Yes, Lord. I'll do anything."

Then I heard the Lord say, "Okay, then, there is something that you must do."

I said, "What, Lord? I'll do anything!"

Then I heard words that were unpleasant and not at all what I wanted to hear: "Ask forgiveness of the youth pastor you offended in your city."

I was shocked! I exclaimed, "Lord, I was right, and he was wrong!"

Of course, I knew I was wrong for saying that. But I wanted to know why I had to be the one to ask for forgiveness!

Then God said, "Go and take Communion with him."

This was not at all what I had imagined when I was asking the Lord to use me. This wasn't easy. It wasn't convenient.

Let me explain. This could not just be a simple text message saying I apologized and then be done with it. When the Lord said I had to take Communion with this brother, I knew He was requiring my heart to be fully engaged. I had to humble myself before God and before this man.

First, I had to call this brother—which took courage—and set up an appointment. Then on the day of my appointment, I had to go to the store and buy bread and juice. After that, I had to travel for over an hour to the appointment.

When I took the first step to call, I was praying he wouldn't answer. But he did answer, and he had an opening for me.

I remember that day well. I did not want to say I was sorry. I did not want to humble myself. I woke up that morning, hoping he would call me to cancel. He did call—but it was to confirm the appointment. God was not letting me off the hook.

Reluctantly, I headed for my meeting with this man. I remember buying a loaf of bread and juice for Communion and then trying unsuccessfully to fit them into my computer bag. In the end, I traveled to the meeting looking extremely odd with a loaf of bread and juice sticking out my bag.

I remember thinking the whole way, *Is this really necessary? Do I really have to embarrass myself and say I'm sorry when I believe I am right?*

I heard God's words in my spirit: "If you want Me to use you, you must ask for forgiveness. I cannot use you until you do this." Meaning if I did not ask for forgiveness and take Communion with this brother, I would not be maximizing the effectiveness of my time of fasting.

Finally, I got to the office of the church where the meeting was to be held. When I walked through the door, many people noticed me. I could see by the expressions on their faces that they were wondering, *Why is he here, and why is he carrying a loaf of bread and juice sticking out of his computer bag?* Some laughed! I felt awkward, but I knew what God had told me to do.

The youth pastor greeted me and asked, "What's on your mind?"

I put the bread and juice on the table and said, "I'm sorry, and I ask your forgiveness. We are the Body of Christ, so let's be examples of unity."

The youth pastor smiled and hugged me; then we took Communion together. It was a wonderful time of fellowship. He is still my friend today and a powerful man of God from whom I am constantly learning.

On my way home from that meeting, I heard God speak to me: "Now I can use you." I was so happy I listened to Him!

The following year I released an album with my band that went viral overnight and blessed multiple countries. I've been told it changed the course of what Russian worship looked like in Russia and in surrounding countries. You can read the full story in my book *Worship Without Limits*. But none of that was because of a gift or talent. God moved in that way because fasting had helped me die to my fleshly preferences in my pursuit to know Him intimately and to please Him completely.

I truly believe that if I hadn't forgiven that pastor and sincerely asked him to forgive me, the future God prepared for me would have been hindered. As we took Communion that day, choosing unity instead of division and strife, that unity commanded the blessing. I received healing through that fast, which changed my heart, aligned me to hear God's voice, and enabled me to act upon what I heard.

We must listen to God's voice and act upon it. Not following the instruction that God gives us during a fast renders the fast almost pointless because it will not produce His desired results in us.

STOMACH HEALED WHILE FASTING

It says in Isaiah 58:8 (NLT), *"your wounds will quickly heal."* I can tell you by my own testimony that this is true. In the beginning of this book, I gave my testimony of healing, but there was one thing I left out. I was diagnosed by the doctors as having gastritis or pus in my stomach. The doctors never told me I should not fast. Of course, they never thought that would be a possibility. I didn't know that I should have consulted a doctor before fasting for an extended time, so I didn't.

Later I found out that fasting with this condition was dangerous. But it was only after my first 40-day fast that I realized I was healed. I could eat whatever I wanted because the Lord had healed me!

Take note, however, that when God heals you, you must keep your healing. In other words, don't do things you know are not wise!

In my case, the fact that I could eat whatever I wanted did not mean that I should eat whatever I wanted. God expected me to exercise discipline. He is merciful and He had healed me, despite my ignorance.

Later as I continued to study fasting, I learned that my healing was actually twofold. I truly believe that the Lord touched me as I fasted. His healing power was working through my entire being. Because I obeyed when I heard His instruction for me to fast, I was in alignment for Him to heal me—but healing was happening on two fronts. God strengthened me spiritually to change my mindset so I could be healed physically.

In short, once your body has been completely flushed out and cleansed, the body no longer needs to digest food that is left over from eating. This normally takes about three to five days.

When you're not fasting, you rest overnight during sleep, but your body is very busy. Through the night, it is digesting food, fighting infection, repairing cells, and strengthening for the next day so that you can be strong. During fasting, your body doesn't need to digest food, but it does keep busy through the night. Instead of processing your food, it focuses on healing your body.

It is not uncommon for stomach issues, dry skin, and eyes to improve or to get healed as a result of fasting. Everything I have just explained to you is just the physical aspect of how wonderfully God designed our bodies to heal themselves.

But remember, I said that my healing took place in two ways. You see, for me I had both the natural and the supernatural working on my behalf. God is so good, and He truly moves in wonderful ways. Both the physical and spiritual worked in concert together so I could receive my full healing.

Use the common sense of a proper diet, plenty of rest, and avoid stress to keep your healing.

BE NOT MOVED BY SOMEONE ELSE'S FAITH

In this point, I must stress one important powerful truth: Fast and pray only as God directs you to. Make sure your motive is right. Fasting done in the flesh as *your* idea and not a *God* idea can be very damaging, even deadly to your body.

Please do not fast just because you read my story about healing. Be inspired by it to go to God and inquire what steps He wants you to take. Then whatever He tells you to do, do it. But take action by faith in God's Word—not in an attempt to imitate another person's experience.

My grandfather was put on dialysis for his kidneys that were not functioning properly. Dialysis is a life sentence. It is done three or four times a week, and there is no way out of it. One day my grandfather was reading the Word of God, and he received revelation about healing. He decided that day that he was healed.

The next day my grandmother told Grandpa to get ready; it was time to go to dialysis. He replied, "I'm not going! I'm healed! The Bible is either true or it's a lie."

My grandfather would not go to dialysis that day. He knew there was a risk of dying if he didn't go, but he could not be moved. Everyone who knew that he was not doing dialysis any longer expected that he would die, but he just continued to live. My grandfather got healed that day. It was a true miracle.

There have been other terrible stories that I have heard of where a minister would come in and tell someone to stop taking their medicine, and as a result they died. In fact, I knew of a case like that in which a teenager died. It was extremely tragic and should not have happened.

What is the difference between my grandfather's healing and a person who was told by someone else not to take the medicine and died? A person truly has to have a word from God. In the case of the girl who stopped taking her medicine, her faith was dependent on the minister, not on God. My grandpa had a true word from God. As Jesus said several times in the Word, "Your faith has made you whole."

I am saying all this to enforce that if you feel you need to fast, you must have a word from God. Do not do it because you are reading this book right now. In my case I got healed from gastritis because I had a word from God to fast, not because I heard someone's message or direction. Don't be moved by someone else's faith. Make sure you have a word from God.

Although I believe with all my heart that you can be healed of various diseases through fasting because of the spiritual and natural effects, you must use wisdom and you must have a word from the Lord. It is possible that God will tell you to do a partial fast of some sort. He might instruct you to practice intermittent fasting. But especially if you are diabetic, you must always ensure that you are using wisdom.

I believe that God can heal you without medicine. I have seen it done in my life. The things that medicine cannot heal, God heals. I also believe that He can use medicine to heal. Many times the doctor will say that it will take a certain number of weeks to get healed, but you can get healed in half that time because the medicine is doing its work and so is God. You get expedited healing because God—not just medicine—is working on your behalf.

God will meet you where your faith is. But trust Him first; then allow doctors and medicine to assist your body in the process.

I want to stress this point one more time: Please use wisdom in this area. Do not fast just because you read a book about fasting—including this one! Fast only because you have a word from God. You can be encouraged by another person's faith or testimony. But do not be moved to take action based on another man's faith. Be moved by a true word from the Lord to you.

Your Standard of Righteousness Grows

Your godliness will lead you forward, and the glory of the Lord will protect you from behind.

Isaiah 58:8 NLT

This scripture says that your godliness will lead you forward. What I have experienced in fasting is that my standard of righteousness grows. Things that I used to tolerate I could no longer tolerate anymore. Things that never grieved me began to grieve me strongly. For example, if I watched a movie, swear words used to not bother me. But when I fasted, they grieved me like never before. Action movies used to not grieve me, but now I can't watch murder and violence.

The same goes for listening to non-Christian music. A simple love song on the radio begins to grieve you, when in times past you didn't even realize that it was on. Watching R-rated movies and listening to the latest trends in music with your friends no longer satisfies you; instead, it grieves your spirit.

Let's go a little deeper! When you hear your friends gossip, you can no longer listen and you just don't enjoy it. It grieves your spirit.

You become very sensitive to words of unbelief that come out of your mouth—words that will destroy your future. These are words you used to say without realizing their negative effect, but now you understand that those very words grieve the Holy Spirit.

The only way that I can explain it to you is that you become super-sensitive. It's like a 4K television. Everything is so clear! You see things you couldn't see in SD or 1080, and it changes you forever. Now you only want to watch in 4K, or you want to buy an even higher definition. You just can't go back to SD.

This is what happens to you when you fast. Your standard of righteousness grows, and you can no longer go back to your old way of living. You realize all the unrighteousness that you allowed through your eyes and ears clogged you up, and now since there is nothing clogging you up, you can hear God's voice so much more clearly.

Fasting and prayer doesn't just change your standard of righteousness during the fast; it changes you—who you are and what you tolerate. Now, of course, you have a choice after the fast. You can choose to change back to who you were. But going back to who you were is a slow process after a fast. The first time you tolerate something that grieved you during the fast, it truly grieves you. Then if you keep doing it over and over again, soon it's like you develop a spiritual callus. It doesn't bother you like it used to. This is the process of backsliding.

Why am I saying all this? Fasting increases your sensitivity to God's voice and causes your standard of righteousness to rise to a new level, but it is not a one-time fix. Fasting will make you stronger, but that doesn't mean that you will never be tempted again. The temptation will come, but through fasting and prayer you become more equipped to deal with it.

Fasting causes you to grow in your walk with the Lord, but this does not mean you negate the most important weapon as a Christian. Living a life of sanctification or a life of spiritual self-discipline is still your greatest weapon.

Praying, fasting, and reading your Bible are all key practices to make part of your lifestyle. But, really, it comes down to making right choices that honor God. Many Christians claim to be wearing the armor of God. But too often those same Christians then allow an open door of access for the enemy by allowing the culture of this world into their lives through movies, games, or music with demonic and perverted influences.

In the discussion above are some key reasons that I encourage you to fast. I know from experience that it will better equip you against attacks from the enemy and direct you in walking into your divine destiny that God has planned for you.

GROWTH IN GOD

Something I have noticed through every fast I have done is that the gifts of the Spirit become stronger in my life. Words of knowledge, words of wisdom, revelations, and dreams from the Lord have become more and more common. I know that some of the songs I have written and messages I have received I would *not* have received had I not been fasting.

Because your sensitivity is stronger to hear God's voice, you are able to see the hidden things. God begins revealing secrets to you. You get spiritual downloads. Isaiah 45:3 becomes a reality, not a fantasy.

> *I will give you hidden treasures, riches stored in secret places, so that you may know that I am the Lord, the God of Israel, who summons you by name.*

Those hidden treasures and riches stored in secret become revealed to you in God's presence as you fast and pray. This is what you can expect in your walk with the Lord. Fasting and praying strengthens your sensitivity to hear His voice so that God's secrets can be revealed to you.

Through all of this, your godliness and new standard of righteousness makes way for you. Doors that were shut begin to open, and favor begins to pour into your life in proportions you did not see prior to that time. Fasting and praying paves the way for the unseen to become seen and the impossible to become possible.

God Hears You When You Cry

> *Then when you call, the Lord will answer. "Yes, I am here," he will quickly reply.*
>
> Isaiah 58:9 NLT

I believe that when you have paid a price of humility, choosing to make your body a living sacrifice, you are sensitized to hear God's voice quickly. Answers come quickly. This happens not because you did something for God or you moved God with your actions or twisted His arm. It occurs because you have chosen to align yourself with God's perfect will, got rid of all distractions, and as a result nothing is blocking you from hearing and receiving His counsel.

Fasting and Praying Reveals
Things on the Inside of Us

> *Remove the heavy yoke of oppression. Stop pointing your finger and spreading vicious rumors! Feed the hungry, and help those in trouble.*
>
> Isaiah 58:9-10 NLT

So many times when I have fasted, God has shown me things that needed to change in me. Often they were things I never thought were there. It's like this: When a metalsmith puts metal under the fire all the impurities come to the surface. Impurities that were unseen now become visible and dislodged for removal.

Our great metalsmith is the King of kings and Lord of lords. When He turns on the fire, hidden impurities rise to the surface. Heavy yokes of oppression start coming off. Embedded things we thought we had dealt with are revealed through the fire. God begins to forge us into His image or have us deal with issues in our character. He starts dealing with us to stop pointing our fingers at others with vicious words and rumors and instead to start dealing with ourselves. This reminds me of what Jesus said: "Why do you look at the speck that is in your brother's eye, but do not notice the log that is in your own eye?" (Matt. 7:3 NASB).

Fasting and praying causes us to fix our own character rather than try to fix everyone else's. Then when God has dealt with us, we can then focus on feeding the hungry and helping those in trouble. He is working on us so that we can be a blessing to others.

Something that is powerful about a metalsmith is that he does not just allow metal to burn and that's it. Instead of just watching it burn, he adds alloys to the metal to make it strong.

Our Great Metalsmith does the same for us. He will not just allow us to burn in the fires of adversity, watching us go through all our fits of carnality. Instead, He adds more love, more mercy, more patience, and more power to us. After all is said and done, through fasting we come to a place where we are no longer judging others. Because we have gone through the transformation of the fire, we are transformed and forged into His likeness through the power of the Blood and the living water of the Word. Because God has performed this miracle in us through His love, we are purified to pour His love into others. Through fasting, a powerful transformation takes place. We stop thinking about ourselves and start thinking about others.

Your Faith Will Shine Stronger Than Ever Before

> *Then your light will shine out from the darkness, and the darkness around you will be as bright as noon.*
>
> Isaiah 58:10 NLT

I can remember doing a 40-day fast while I lived in Moscow, Russia. I was on day 30, and mentally I was preparing to go to jazz school. In jazz school, I knew that I would have to do vocal classes, which take a lot of energy. I knew that I would have to push myself. I knew that even though my stomach hurt and I felt fatigued, I would have to smile and say to everyone, "I'm doing great!" As all of this was reality, I asked the Lord if He would allow me not to do a 40-day fast but to stop at 30 days so I would be stronger for all my vocal lessons and not look like a freak in front of my classmates.

Let me clarify something. Most people think that singing is not work. In short, singing and leading worship, if you do it right, will take a lot of physical work. To project your voice correctly, you have to use your diaphragm—and the truth is, you feel more strength in that muscle when you've had a nice meal. And if you haven't eaten for 30 days, singing can be difficult. This is why I was expecting God would say, "Good job! You have done enough already! Stop at 30!"

His answer was a little different than I had planned. He said, "Philip, you can do whatever you want, but the full blessing that I have planned for you is if you do the full 40 days." I knew that I wanted to keep my word to God, so I continued.

MIRACLE IN JAZZ SCHOOL

The first day at school, everything that I expected to happen did happen, and much more. I can remember my first lesson. My teacher asked if I was tired. She said that it seemed that I could project more with my voice. She asked if everything was okay. Normally, I do not tell everyone that I am fasting, but I asked the Lord about it and He said to go ahead.

I replied to her, "I am fasting."

She said, "Great! Are you doing the Russian Orthodox fast? How long you been doing it?" (A Russian Orthodox fast happens once a year. You are allowed to buy holy eggs, sausage, and other designated foods.)

My teacher asked me what kind of foods I was eating for my Orthodox fast.

I replied, "No, it's not Orthodox, and I am not eating anything. I'm just drinking liquids."

The teacher was shocked. "Why would you do that?" she asked. "How long is this fast?"

I said, "For 40 days. Today is day 33." I explained, "I love God, and I just want to draw near to Him and bless Him. So I am offering this up to Him as a sacrifice, showing Him that

I love Him more than I do necessary food. Instead of using the time I would use for breakfast, lunch, and dinner, I use that time to pray and spend time with the Lord while drinking only liquids."

The teacher had a look of astonishment on her face. I was actually a little astonished that I gave her such an in-depth response, but it seemed right to do. In that moment, I wasn't sure if I had shocked her and she thought I was a weirdo or she respected me for it.

Then my teacher replied, "That's awesome! I respect you so much for that! That's what this generation needs—someone who loves God with all their heart, even more than food!"

The next class was drama, or acting. The teacher got up and said, "Here is your assignment. You need to get up in front of class right now and demonstrate confidence. You must recite a poem from Dostoevsky or Pushkin."

Everyone got up and recited something, and the whole time I was thinking, I don't know poems from Dostoevsky or Pushkin. What am I going to do? All I knew in Russian was Psalm 91.

Quoting might be a little awkward, but it could be a way for my faith to shine. I knew this was my moment. I got up and said, "I can quote the Bible!" The teacher looked at me with astonishment and said, "Okay, go for it!" I started as if I were telling a story. Imagine the 91st Psalm being spoken in a commanding Russian voice!

He that dwelleth in the secret place of the most High shall abide under the shadow of the Almighty. I will say of the Lord, He is my refuge

*and my fortress: my God; in Him will I trust. Surely
he shall deliver thee from the snare of the fowler,
and from the noisome pestilence.*

I added more drama and suspense, and I had everyone's
attention. They had never seen anyone act out the Bible or
even heard Psalm 91 before! After I was done, I could feel the
room was in shock! I sat down right next to my classmate. He
looked at me, astounded, and said, *"What was that?* I need
to go get coffee with you. You are weird, but I like you."

After classes that day, I had the opportunity to preach to
my classmate. Pretty soon my whole class was talking about
the weird Christian who fasted. It was the best gossip ever!
I was weird to them but holy to God, and my behavior was
causing God's light to shine! My fasting that day caused a
chain reaction to happen in that school! It was awesome.

I remember another day I came to my vocal lesson, and
my stomach was hurting. I also felt fatigued and very dizzy.
I was dreading my lesson that day because I was in so much
pain. When I walked into the door, my teacher said, "You are
glowing. There is such a presence around you!" I knew that it
had to be God in His mercy working on her heart, because I
was feeling horrible. Yet through my weakness, Christ's light
was revealing His power and glory. I replied, "It's not me, It's
all Him!"

So many things happened in that school. I can remember how people would tell me, "Don't sing Christian songs
on your exam because the judges won't like it. They will give
you a bad grade."

I'd respond, "Singing a Christian song is worth my getting a bad grade. I'm going to sing about God, no matter what!"

Not only did I sing Christian songs on my exam, but the anointing would touch the judges and my classmates. Fellow students would wipe away their tears because of God's presence, and the judges would ask, "What was that aura that was around you? What is the influence behind your music?"

My reply was always, "It's not me. It's Jesus!"

Then the judges would give me the best grade I could get!

When you stand up for God, God will always stand up for you!

I saw many demonstrations of God's power during my time attending that jazz school, but the greatest testimony happened after I left. For years I prayed for my vocal teacher to give her life to the Lord, and it did not happen. I fasted and prayed for her and her daughter. I cried out to God for them to be saved. After I finished school, someone asked me to share the contact information of the best vocal teacher I knew.

I answered, "I'll give it to you, but on one condition. Bring her to church and get her saved."

Two years later, both my former voice teacher and her daughter gave their lives to the Lord. As I think back to all this, it's absolutely amazing that it all started with a day of fasting. It is very possible that I would not have experienced these testimonies if had I not fasted that week. During that fast, I was expecting open doors and new songs. Well, I got that and so much more! I was thinking about what God could do for me, but God was thinking about souls impacted for the Kingdom.

I have shared these stories to prove Isaiah 58:10—that through fasting, your light will shine in the darkness and the world will recognize that it is not you but the power of God that is inside you. Fasting and prayer causes you to shine like never before.

Always Supernaturally Refreshed

> *The Lord will guide you continually, giving you water when you are dry and restoring your strength. You will be like a well-watered garden.*
> Isaiah 58:11 NLT

Something I find amazing is that although there are days as you fast when you are exhausted and very hungry, there are also days when you feel such a surge of strength that you know it's not natural for you to feel like that. Your logic begins to talk to you: *You haven't eaten in what seems forever! How can you feel so good?*

Almost every 40-day fast I have done, I have finished with a three-hour worship service on day 39. I do not plan this, but somehow it happens. This should be impossible, because a diaphragm that has had no nourishment for an extended period of time should not be able to project vocally. But those nights of worship have been some of the easiest ever. There is a grace that comes on me that makes the impossible possible. Let me explain.

Like everything that God calls us to do, there is a grace for it, and fasting and praying are no exception. There should be no way that you could sing for three hours on the 39th day of fasting, yet this has happened to me almost every single time. The reason for it is that it's not my talent but God's grace that pulls me through. Regardless of the duration, there is a grace on a 40-, 30-, 10-, 7-, 3-, or 1-day fast. If God has given you a mandate to fast, rest assured there will be a grace on you to fulfill the assignment with flying colors.

Second Corinthians 12:9 blesses me because it proves that in my weakness, God is strong. Many times, I would tell my worship team, "We are fasting today." Of course, that evening would be the night of worship.

My team would say, "Cool! We will fast all day and eat right before sound check; then we will be strong for the worship night."

My reply would be, "No, we will eat after the worship night. We play in our weakness. Then when we see people getting healed and touched by God's power, we will know it is not because of our strength but because His grace manifested through our weakness made us strong in Him."

Afterward, I'd ask the guys how they felt. They'd reply, "I felt tired and weak, but then God's strength came on me, and I knew that it just wasn't me playing, that it was God playing through my hands."

This is a powerful principle that can be applied in any arena of life. If you will trust and rely upon God in your weakness, His grace is sufficient to makes you strong in Him.

This applies to every area—sports, the workplace, music, business, etc. When you make the decision that you are not afraid, fast and still go on with your daily life. In your weakness God will make you strong!

REBUILDING WHAT WAS LOST AND RAISING THE NEXT GENERATION

> *Some of you will rebuild the deserted ruins of your cities. Then you will be known as a rebuilder of walls and a restorer of homes.*
>
> Isaiah 58:12 NLT

I fully realize that everything that has happened to me in ministry is not a result of my talent or life experiences. The truth is, we are all a result of the prayers, faith, and obedience of others who have gone before us to pave a path, starting with the heroes of Hebrews 11. They never saw the power of the New Covenant activated. They never saw Jesus die on the Cross and gain victory over death, yet they prayed and fasted for it. They never saw the Holy Spirit poured out on all flesh. They prophesied it, preached it, and died for it, yet they never saw it. You and I stand as the product of their prophecies, their lives, their fasting, and their faith that still speaks before God.

> *These were all commended for their faith, yet none of them received what had been promised, since God had planned something better for us so that only together with us would they be made perfect.*
>
> Hebrews 11:39-40

PRAYER PAVES THE WAY FOR
THE NEXT GENERATION

The heroes of the Old Testament never saw what you and I live in daily. Moses fasted for 40 days and saw the hand of God write the 10 commandments that formed the very moral fabric of what we live by today. Joshua was on the same mountain during his fast. It is a powerful representation of passing the fire from one generation to the next. This caused the power of God to be manifested through the nations and God's Kingdom plan to be activated for the Savior of the world to be born.

Fasting is powerful! Fasting paves the way! Hundreds of years earlier, another man was fasting and paving the way for Moses. In Jentezen Franklin's book *Fasting*, he mentions that Joseph fasted and prayed in prison. You see, it was not uncommon for prisoners not to be fed while in prison. Joseph was thrown in prison after being wrongly accused of sleeping with Potiphar's wife. It is not a coincidence that Joseph received the wisdom of God concerning how to navigate the coming famine during times of fasting and prayer.

Joseph received wisdom that caused him to save his family (even a nation!) from certain death. Joseph saved the future nation of God's people from whom Moses and then Joshua would be born to lead. Finally, David would become the greatest king in the history of the Jewish people—a man after God's own heart. David was the only man in the Bible to be given that kind of title. It would then be through this man's family line that Jesus would be born to save the world from sin and free us from Satan's kingdom.

Joseph's prayers paved the way for Moses, David, and Jesus to be born. And before that, Enoch's life of righteousness paved the way for Noah, Abraham, Jacob, and Isaac.

You see, we are all a result of someone else's life and prayers.

The Renner family has seen the Lord do great things in Russia. Some would say that my father moving to Russia with his family was a catalyst for revival. This is true, but my dad and our family are not the only ones who paid a great price. Consider the thousands of Russian believers who died in concentration camps or gulags for the Gospel.

Ella's grandfather was one of those sent to prison for the Gospel in Soviet Russia. Imprisoned for their faith, Russian believers prayed for the day when they could have Christian programs on secular Russian television. They prayed for the day when the Bible would be sold in bookstores and potentially be in every Russian home. They prayed for religious freedom in Russia and all the countries of the former Soviet Union. They prayed for a sound of worship to arise from those countries. Imagine that this is what these Russian believers prayed at a time when they were possibly about to be executed for their faith!

In prison believers were often not fed adequately, so they'd make a choice to fast and pray to see revival and religious freedom become a reality. Many of them died shortly afterward and never got to see the manifestation of what they prayed for, but that doesn't mean their prayers were not accurate or effective.

Today we are walking in what these believers prayed and died for.

My point is this: Prayers have always gone before us. You are a result of someone else's fasting and praying. The book that I am writing right now is a result of someone praying for it. It is through this kind of prayer that the Kingdom plans of God are activated.

Prayer Like a Shield

When I was 16, I was living a life that was a form of godliness but not true godliness. No one really knew what was going on, but my mom was praying for me.

One morning on the way from a men's breakfast, the driver started driving recklessly. He wanted to show off his new car. The problem was, the road was so icy that when he accelerated in speed from 20 to 80 miles per hour within a matter of seconds the car spun out of control and we hit two large concrete posts. Metal railings were in between those posts—and to top it all off, we hit a light pole and bent it. This all happened by the Moscow River.

As I got out of the car, I realized I should be either dead from the accident or drowned in the river. We should have not bounced off the metal railings; we should have gone straight through them and into the river!

The other thing that I realized was the car should have been completely destroyed. Although it looked smashed on the back and front, the car didn't blow up—and the spot where my brother and I were sitting was completely untouched! I knew this was nothing short of a miracle. The next thing I noticed left me speechless.

At the moment of impact, the driver's seat broke. As it broke, a piece of metal shot forward from the engine and went out the back windshield. Had the driver's seat not broken and shifted backward, the piece of metal would have shot straight through his body!

All three of us in that car understood we should have been killed. Prayer surrounded us with angelic protection.

A couple of days later, my family passed that same place at the Moscow River site and a wreck similar to ours had just taken place—only this time, the police were zipping up three body bags. I was gripped by the sight of that image. I knew that those three body bags could have been for the three of us. I also knew that the only reason I was saved that day was that my mom was fasting and praying for me. I don't doubt that others were praying for me as well, but I know Mom was praying for me. My backslidden hidden life, my form of godliness with no power, had opened the door for the enemy to infiltrate my life, but my mom's fasting and praying stopped his ability to destroy me.

My point is this: Fasting and praying causes you to raise up the next generation. Many times as I fast, I get into a place in the Spirit where I know I am praying for future evangelists, preachers, pastors, prophets, and apostles. Fasting and praying rips them out of the grip of hell's intent and directs them on a path of true righteousness.

King David was a man who fasted, and he understood this:

So the next generation would know them, even the children yet to be born, and they in turn would tell their children. Then they would put their trust in God and would not forget his deeds but would keep his commands. They would not be like their ancestors—a stubborn and rebellious generation, whose hearts were not loyal to God, whose spirits were not faithful to him.

Psalm 78:6-8

Notice this phrase *"children yet to be born."* In Hebrews 11, the heroes of the Bible never saw what was promised to them. Yet they impacted the next generation; they impacted the children yet to be born.

When you fast and pray, you are impacting not only this generation, but your prayer also goes into a place that transcends time, and you pray in those who have great destiny. You pray in the "children yet to be born." Not only is that true, but according to Isaiah 58:12, you also rebuild what the enemy planned to be destroyed.

Through fasting and prayer, we rebuild lives that our adversary planned to destroy.

Through fasting and prayer, we birth dreams in the hearts of people that had been aborted by the enemy.

By living a fasted lifestyle, your life becomes a prayer. Your life becomes a continual expression of worship to the Father, as well as an expression of the Father's heart to people. Because you have taken time to know your God, He makes you strong to do exploits for the glory of His name.

As a yielded vessel, a new wineskin continually filled with the new wine of His Spirit, you will carry the presence of God into situations and allow Him to overflow. You will be known as one who does your part to ransom the souls of men. You will be known as one who rebuilds walls of protection around people's lives. The Bible calls it being a "repairer of the breach" (see Isa. 58:12) for those who need shelter from the storms of life and from the deadly attacks of the devil.

As an able laborer whom the Lord trusts to bring in His harvest, you will walk as one to establish the total restoration into the homes the enemy tried to destroy. He tried but he was unsuccessful because of your prayers released through your life poured out in selfless service to God and to people.

This is the power of fasting and praying. This is the power of a life that's willing to yield to and work in the unseen realm of God in prayer. God makes you a promise. What you have yielded up to Him in private will be rewarded publicly before men for His glory.

MY PRAYER

Father God, I thank You for teaching me how to enter fully into the power of a fasted life. I choose a lifestyle of consecration and surrender to You. My pursuit is to know You, to be strong in You, and to be an instrument You can use to manifest Your power to set the captives free.

Make me a new wineskin, overflowing with the new wine of Your Spirit every day so that my life will cause people to drink from Your living water, to taste and see that You are good. I ask You to cause compassion to grow inside me and to conform my character to reveal Your holy standards so the light of Your glory and righteousness will shine bright in me.

Holy Spirit, teach me to do my part to strengthen this generation, to win the lost, and to exalt the name of Jesus higher and higher so that all might see and receive Him as Savior, Lord, and soon-coming King. Purify my heart; help me keep my motives right. Father God, help me to honor and obey You fully in all things. I seek Your heart, not Your hand. And I stand before You as a son who serves, giving You all that I am, withholding nothing.

Jesus, You are my everything. Thank You for strengthening me to walk in Your ways forever. In the name of Jesus, I pray. Amen.

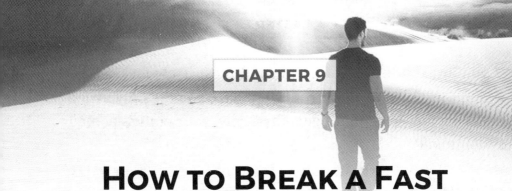

CHAPTER 9

HOW TO BREAK A FAST

IT IS MY hope that in this book, I have established spiritual points about the value of fasting and prayer to help you deepen your relationship with God. But now I would like to address some practical matters that will help you make wise choices as you end your fast.

I believe that the way you break a fast and resume eating again is where you are truly tested. I also believe that you can get just as much breakthrough in breaking the fast with honor as you do during the fast.

For me personally, I have received an equal amount of revelation during the fast and in breaking the fast correctly. God has spoken to me coming out of a fast just as much as He has spoken to me when I am in a fast.

All through the fast, your mind is telling you to eat—but you can control your flesh. Honestly, the most challenging time of a fast can be on day four or five. This is when you might deal with stomachaches, headaches, dizziness, fatigue, or feeling sleepy. This happens because your body is detoxing, getting rid of all the junk you have put in it, and as a result you do not feel well. But just wait it out. When you awaken the next day you will most likely feel like you don't want to eat at all. You will realize you are only experiencing thoughts of hunger. Physically, your body is actually doing well.

As I previously stated, a grace comes upon you to fast. This does not mean that you will have no difficult days. You will have them. But it is not because you actually need food. The struggle is in the realm of your thoughts as you control your flesh. Requiring your flesh to be quiet and refusing to let it control you is the fight when you fast. When you conquer your cravings and thoughts, your spirit subdues your flesh, gaining power over yourself—and that is true victory.

THE STRUGGLE IS REAL!

Your own thoughts will oppose your obedience to fast—especially when your friends invite you to dinner and they have prepared your favorite meal. You think to yourself, *Why couldn't they have invited me over a week ago when I could have enjoyed that barbeque, that lasagna, that steak dinner?* Instead, you sit at the table, watching everyone else eat. People ask if you're okay, and you just smile and say, "I'm doing great!"

You're wrestling, determined to control your own flesh. You may feel weak, but you're increasing in spiritual strength and gaining power. It's not fun; it's a real fight. But the results are transformation and the anointing that comes only by conquering your flesh as you stay committed to what the Lord has told you to do.

Yes, you will have several of these days on a fast. They are inevitable. During those days, you may look at food and feel provoked to think, *The minute the clock strikes 12 am and I complete my fast, I will eat everything I want!* Trust me, that is a huge mistake.

I say that from personal experience because I have made some stupid mistakes while fasting. No one really taught me how to fast correctly, so I learned the hard way. When I began my journey in fasting, I did not have a book that explained the importance of ending a fast correctly. I learned by falling on my face—a lot.

I told you in Chapter 1 about the first time I fasted for a week when I was 14 years old. I knew the exact minute and hour that I started fasting. So in my mind I already had a game plan of how I was going to stop.

THE WRONG WAY TO BREAK A FAST

I was living in Riga, Latvia, at the time, and there was an amazing cafe in the downtown area that sold all kinds of crepes. My favorite was caramel banana chocolate. So I timed my arrival there precisely. I waited for the exact minute and hour that I had started the fast a week earlier. As soon as the hand on the clock hit the right hour, I thought, *Ready, set, go!*

Well, go I did! Driven more by the memory of how hungry I felt during the fast, I inhaled at least ten of those banana caramel chocolate crepes—and then immediately reached for something different! I quickly devoured some strawberry chocolate crepes; then I ate a cookie, followed by a large Coke!

Some of my friends were with me, cheering me on: "Look at Philip go! Wow! He finished his first fast—let's party! Eat another one!" They were happy that I made it through and could eat again. All I was thinking was, *Finally, I've got some food in my mouth!*

But there were a few friends who asked me, "Are you sure you should be eating that much so soon?"

Little did I know that their caution was the voice of wisdom. Meanwhile, the voice of common sense was rising up inside me, telling me, "Don't be stupid! Stop! You are committing the sin of gluttony!" The prompting to stop was strong, but I ignored it and instead said, "Give me some more!"

At first, I felt great—but then it hit me. I felt like I was going to throw up. By the time I got home, it felt as though a bomb had exploded in my stomach. I felt horrible and I was constipated for three to four days. I told myself I would never do that again—or so I thought. I was wrong. I continued to make mistakes. I had to learn how to break a fast correctly.

The second fast that I did was a two-week fast on liquids. I didn't prepare for that fast properly. So although I completed it, I experienced much discomfort. Again, I was counting the hours for it to be over with no plan to exercise self-control. At first, I tried by starting with salad. But then I somehow progressed to 14 Snickers candy bars!

I'm embarrassed even now as I admit that, but it's true. That's where I was in my understanding at the time. I learned by falling down. But that is one of the reasons I'm writing this book—I want you to avoid the mistakes I made through lack of knowledge. I encourage you to consult your doctor or healthcare professional for qualified medical advice. But I hope this book will help equip you with spiritual and practical principles that help you realize the importance of breaking your fast according to wisdom.

When I finally got clear that I was to do my first 40-day fast, by that time I understood that I would need to come out of it slowly. I decided that I needed to come out of it over the course of three days. Of course, I did not know that this was not enough time. It should have been more like three to four weeks.

After 40 days without food, instead of consuming nutrient-rich clear broths, which is best, I resumed eating. I began with salads for a day, then the next day I moved to crackers because there were a ton available at the youth retreat I was attending. That same day, I also ate meat pies. Soon I felt pain in my stomach like no other. I vomited and had diarrhea at the same time.

I don't mean to be crude, but I want to be real with you. You need to know the results of breaking a fast incorrectly. I did it all wrong, and I suffered the consequences for it physically. It was then I repented before God. I knew I needed knowledge of how to do this without harming my stomach in the process. People have been known to die from eating steak after coming out of a long fast. That is why I encourage you to consult qualified medical professionals.

The Bible says that we are the temple of the Holy Spirit. Here is the truth: You get only one temple, one body, so you must take care of it. You were bought with a great price; therefore, you are to glorify God with your body (see 1 Cor. 6:19-20).

Fasting is an opportunity that not only can change you spiritually but also can change your lifestyle. If you listen to the Holy Spirit, He will give you direction about changes that you need to make in every area of your life. He may even tell you it's time for you to exercise on a regular basis. Imagine going to stand in a prayer line and receiving that as the word of knowledge to possess your healing!

I remember the day God spoke to me and said, "Philip, if I ask you to preach five times in a day when you are eighty-five, will you be able to do it?"

I replied, "No, Lord!"

"Then start working out. I need your body strong!"

That was what the Lord told me. He might tell you something different, but this is my story.

God will speak to you during and after a fast. It is your decision to listen to Him or to ignore Him. Many times people will say, "I did not change during a fast." That is not my experience.

I am speaking generally, but if you didn't change during a fast, it wasn't because God wasn't speaking to you. It is simply because you ignored what He was saying. You can go through a 40-day fast, and God will speak to you constantly. But if you're not listening with your spiritual ears and doing what He tells you, nothing will happen. Nothing will change.

Change is up to us! Through ignoring God's instructions, we reduce a powerful time with the Lord to religious tradition, which is powerless.

A fast is not like a "pill" you take that will make everything right. Throughout a fast and afterward, you have to make lifestyle changes. Whether those changes be physical or spiritual, the choice is up to you to change! God can't do that for you. That is your responsibility.

PROTECT YOUR BODY—YOU ONLY GET ONE!

You can read the Bible and know that your body is the temple of the Holy Spirit, yet completely ignore that truth. If you do, there will be consequences—not because the Word of God didn't work, but because your unbelief to take action made the Word powerless.

The opposite is also true, and that is good news. If you apply what God is telling you through a fast, it will completely change your life and even your lifestyle. Your obedience will maximize the power of what God wanted to do in your life.

Obedience to the Lord's instruction is key, not only when fasting but throughout every day of our lives.

In the following section, I will share with you what God taught me about how to come out of a fast. I'm excited to share it with you. And if you apply these guidelines, you will protect your body.

Your body is the temple of the Holy Spirit and your authorization to operate on the earth. I can't remind you enough: Protect your body—you only get one!

PRACTICAL ADVICE

I began to research the correct way to come out of a fast, and I found that this is the golden rule to follow: *However long you fast, that's the same amount of time it should take to break the fast.*

You might say, "Philip, that is hard! If I have fasted for a week, I want to eat everything in sight when the fast ends. My stomach is screaming, 'Give me food!' I have been dreaming of my favorite meal for a week, and now is my moment!"

I understand this well. I have been there many times, but let me explain the physical and spiritual reasons why breaking a fast correctly is the best decision. Let's start with the physical side.

Many people instead of losing weight or feeling better after a fast actually feel worse and gain more weight as a result. Then they blame the fast and say, "Fasting isn't for me. I can't do it."

That's simply not true. It's like saying, "This car is bad because I ran a stoplight and got into a wreck with it." That's nonsense. You got in a wreck because you didn't use common sense when you were driving, not because the car is bad.

The same is true with breaking a fast. Many people are worse off after the fast than they were before because they didn't use common sense in breaking it. The truth is, in America and other Western nations, we are addicted to food that has mostly no nutritional value and is high in calories. We could all benefit from a "reset," and there are some practical ways to do this.

LEARN TO PROCESS FOOD AGAIN

As you fast, your body is not processing food. As a result, your stomach shrinks over a period of time. In your mind, you may think you can eat as usual, but you can't because your body was not made to force your stomach to stretch out again. It must be done gradually over time. If it's not done like this, your body will go into shock. It will try to process all the food, but it can't, so a lot of it is turned into fat, resulting in you gaining weight, feeling horrible, and often becoming constipated.

Obviously, this is not a medical description of what occurs. I'm sharing my own experience. Unfortunately, I have experienced this many times—and trust me, it is not worth it. Your body is the temple of the Holy Spirit. You only get one, so take care of it and use it correctly.

I finally learned that when I'm fasting, I will ask the Lord to guide me and help me break the fast correctly. I am so thankful He does.

One of the things that I do to rebuild my body in fasting is take multivitamins and work out. This helps me feel better and disciplines me. Honestly, fasting has changed my life habits.

I believe that when coming out of a fast correctly, your taste buds change. You haven't had food that is bad for you in a long time, so in that detoxification process you have also forgotten the taste. Then when you have a bite of something that truly is not good for you, your body will signal you that what you just put in your mouth was a poor choice!

Have you ever gotten off of sugar for a month and then eaten food that has sugar? Things you never thought were sweet seem extremely sweet because you haven't been used to it. Then as time goes by and you get used to eating sugar again, you become numbed once more to its taste. Through the fast, your body got cleansed from all that junk, but you're back to putting more in. Of course, if you continue to eat foods with sugar, you will start wanting more because you've become numb to its effect once again.

I remember one 40-day fast that I went on in particular. I had made the decision that I would come out of it correctly, which meant I needed to break the fast over the course of another 40 days. It was week four or five on coming out of that fast when my friends invited me to eat with them. They said, "Philip, we have some awesome fish soup." I hate fish, but I did not want to offend my friends so I decided to eat the soup. I felt disgusted looking at the bits of fish in the soup, but I was ready to endure it out of respect. Then to my surprise, I loved it! I wanted more of it. I think I had three bowls of it, it was so good!

I was shocked by how much I enjoyed that soup. I wondered what had happened. Then the realization hit me that because I had been coming out of the fast so slowly my taste buds were reset, and because fish is good for my body, my body responded well to it. And to this day, I like fish!

Practical Tips from My Personal Experience

I am not a medical expert on nutrition. I share these tips from my personal experience. No one gave me a book to read about breaking a fast correctly. I learned the hard way. I know what it's like to have experienced fasts where I gained weight and was worse off than when I started. I have also experienced fasts that have changed my diet in a good way.

First, here are a few important general guidelines. Before you begin a fast, it helps to prepare your body with intermittent fasting and lighter meals. I have found that helps with a smoother transition.

When breaking different kinds of fasts:

- Always consult your doctor and nutritionist.
- Do not attempt heavy food after a liquid-only fast, or it can have serious consequences.
- During recovery, drink juice that is not as acidic by mixing with water. This works well with your stomach.
- I suggest freshly made juice and water with a pH balance of 7.5 and higher.
- Throughout the breaking of any fast, always listen to your body. It will send you signals of what is good or bad for you to eat.

SUGGESTED RECOVERY DIET FOR A 3-DAY LIQUIDS OR WATER-ONLY FAST

- Day 1: Diluted juice (water and juice mix of 30%, 50%, 70%, and then 100% juice).
- Day 2: Salads, fruits, and protein shakes.
- Day 3: Light meals of your choice—chicken, fish, etc.

SUGGESTED RECOVERY DIET FOR
A 7-DAY LIQUIDS FAST

- Day 1: Cream of wheat massages your stomach and wakes it up two to three times a day. Drink lots of water!

- Day 2: Fruits. The easiest fruits to process are bananas and baked apples. Drink lots of water!

- Day 3: Vegetables, fruits, cream of wheat, protein shakes. Drink lots of water!

- Day 4: Vegetables, fruits, bread, pasta, cheese, dairy products, protein shakes. Drink lots of water!

- Day 5: Vegetables, fruits, bread, cheese, dairy products, fish (one of the easiest proteins to process). Drink lots of water!

- Day 6: Vegetables, fruits, bread, cheese, dairy products, fish, chicken, nuts. Drink lots of water!

- Day 7: Vegetables, fruits, bread, cheese, dairy products, fish, chicken, nuts, sweets. Drink lots of water!

SUGGESTED RECOVERY DIET FOR A 40-DAY FAST

Note: Always consult your doctor and nutritionist before attempting this fast.

Warning: Do not attempt to eat heavy food during recovery from a long fast, or it could have serious consequences.

- Week 1: Cream of wheat two to three times a day massages your stomach and wakes it up. Continue to drink lots of water and warm broth.
- Week 2: Fruits. The easiest fruits to process are bananas and baked apples. Drink lots of water!
- Week 3: Vegetables, fruits, cream of wheat. Drink lots of water!
- Week 4: Vegetables, fruits, bread, pasta, cheese, dairy products, protein shakes. Drink lots of water!
- Week 5: Vegetables, fruits, bread, cheese, dairy products, fish (one of the easiest proteins to process). Drink lots of water!
- Week 6: Vegetables, fruits, bread, cheese, diaries, fish, chicken, nuts. Drink lots of water!
- Week 7: Vegetables, fruits, bread, cheese, diaries, fish, chicken, nuts, sweets. Drink lots of water!

Remember, *always listen to your body.* It will send you signals of what is good and bad.

Following this or a similar plan, you can lose weight and change your eating habits, which will change your lifestyle. Although the point of a fast is not to lose weight, coming out of a fast correctly will equip you for change spiritually as well as physically. Through breaking a fast correctly, you are exercising self-control and continually crucifying your flesh, which is a commandment from God.

My Suggested Fasting Guidelines

Through my own experience, I have discovered the following guidelines to be very helpful:

1. Drink lots of water. You must be hydrated during a fast. (Drinks with caffeine are not recommended; caffeine dehydrates.)

2. The toughest time of a fast will usually be the third and fourth day. Your body is flushing out toxins that are being released through headaches, dizziness, and fatigue. By the fifth day, your body will adjust and it will get easier.

3. Days when you feel pain or lack of strength are usually because you are losing weight, not because you are getting sick. (Go pray, and you will be refreshed.) Consult a doctor if needed.

4. Never drink dairy, such as milk, followed by acidic drinks, such as orange juice. This causes a very painful explosion in the stomach.

5. Drink quality water with a pH balance of 7.5 and higher and quality juice (preferably freshly squeezed juices or organic).

6. Drink mainly room temperature water or warm water so that your body is not wasting energy heating it up as it processes it.

7. On extended fasts, your body core will not heat itself without food. There will be days when you will feel cold even when it's hot outside or inside. Drink a hot broth to warm your body.

8. Don't fight your body whenever you feel the need to sleep, even briefly; it is necessary for strength. The amount of time you will actually sleep during the fast will be reduced overall because your body won't require as much.

9. Because your body does not need to process food during a fast, it focuses on healing your body instead. It is not uncommon for skin, eyes, inflammation, and stomach illnesses to be healed during a fast.

10. Life responsibilities, such as taking care of your family, work, and church, do not stop. You continue it all just as if you had all the strength in the world.

11. Physical exercise during a fast is beneficial up to two weeks. Work out to maintain strength, not to build it. Do not overexert yourself.

12. Journal during a fast and after you break a fast. You will be shocked by how much you

will be aware of God speaking to you during and after a fast.

13. Just as you prepare to help your body adjust and begin a fast, prepare to end your fast. Breaking a fast should happen gradually. **Important rule**: The time devoted to breaking the fast should be as long as the duration of the fast itself.

14. Correctly breaking a fast will change your habits and your diet; it will change *you* body, soul, and spirit.

15. Work out after a fast gradually. Taking vitamins with a proper diet reboots and strengthens your system.

16. Consult your doctor if you have any current health conditions before attempting a fast. Use wisdom and proceed in wisdom, not foolishness.

17. The length of a fast is based on level of faith and what God has called you to. Be honest with yourself and how prepared your body, soul, and spirit are.

18. Common sense is that you attempt a 3-day fast before you attempt a 21-day fast. Long fasts can have serious consequences to your body if not done correctly.

19. A supernatural or dry fast is only for the spiritually mature and is to be initiated by God,

not you or others. Remember: God isn't moved by the length or type of your fast. Fasting changes you; it does not force God to move on your behalf.

20. Your family is important. Do not cause emotional harm to yourself or to your family or others. Walk in a spirit of humility, regardless of whether or not friends and family understand your journey.

GOD WILL CONTINUE TO SPEAK TO YOU AFTER THE FAST

Something I have noticed is that God continually speaks to me even after a fast. Something I practice and have found helpful is journaling. I encourage you to journal everything that God speaks to you during a fast. It will also benefit you to continue journaling even as you're coming out of the fast.

In other words, if I am fasting for one week, I will journal what God says to me for seven days. Then when breaking the fast, I continue to journal for another seven days. The interesting thing is that I can actually sense God changing my heart more in breaking the fast than during the fast.

As you break the fast, God will continue to speak to you. Your self-control will be strengthened; your eating habits will change; your health will improve; and you will lose weight.

SELF-CONTROL

I know what it's like when you fast for a week and you want to immediately eat everything in sight when it's over. So you break the fast unwisely, feel horrible afterward, and then tell yourself you'll never do that again.

I have also been in situations when I broke a 40-day all-water fast with broth only and one week later had only worked up to eating baby food because that was all I could consume at that moment. Starting off even with baby food would have been way too heavy for my stomach. Eating baby food felt embarrassing to me, but through it all, God was teaching me self-control.

I remember that it was about four weeks into breaking that same fast that my wife made macaroni and meatballs. I wanted it so badly! So to save myself from yielding to temptation, I went into the bathroom, looked in the mirror, and told myself, "Philip, you are stronger than your desire to eat the macaroni your wife made for the kids. Get it together!" I even said out loud, "I rebuke you, macaroni!"

Now, it's not very biblical to rebuke macaroni—but it worked for me. At that moment, it felt like my kids' macaroni was talking to me, so I had to talk back! Eating macaroni and meatballs at that point could have hurt my stomach. I won that day, and my little pep talk in the mirror helped me. Everyone has his or her own ways of getting through moments of temptation like that, and that was my way in that particular situation.

I remember the first time I ever fasted for 40 days. I was on day 38, and my wife said she was inviting all our friends to the house for barbecue. My first reaction was, *That will be torture!* But since Ella hadn't been able to enjoy friends coming for a visit at our home for almost 40 days and she wanted to have fun, I said, "Sure, that would be great."

Honestly, I didn't believe she would do it, but then came the food and guests. It was really happening. I was dreading it. I could imagine the scenario, looking at all my friends eating barbecue with sauce all over their mouths while I smiled like nothing was wrong.

Then with a mouthful of food, someone would ask, "Philip, are you hungry?"

I would avoid saying how I really felt and just reply, "No, thank you. I'm fine." I was not looking forward to that scenario.

As they all gathered and stuffed themselves, I just smiled and drank my juice. My stomach felt like it was screaming, "Eat!" But I sensed the Lord encouraging me, "Philip, stay steady for just two more days. Be faithful!"

I also knew that my stomach had shrunk and wouldn't be able to process meat. I reminded myself that my stomach needed to be retaught slowly. The stretching of my stomach would have to be a slow process. That is what breaking a fast correctly is.

I also knew that eating meat at that moment would be like throwing a brick in a running car engine. The engine would explode.

That's what would have happened if I had broken the fast incorrectly. I had heard stories of Christians who had broken a 40-day fast incorrectly and died as a result. So I knew that if

I broke the fast by eating heavy food on the 38th day, I would basically be saying, "I love food more than my family. Even if this food kills me, I'm going to eat it." I knew that if I ate that food, I could be saying goodbye to my family.

This may seem dramatic, but the temptation was so strong. I knew if I broke the fast then, I would not stop and I'd hurt myself in the process. So instead, I got up, excused myself from the table, went to my room, and cried.

Then I prayed, "God, empty me of my hunger. Empty me of myself. Empty me of my dreams, and give me Your dreams."

First, I prayed it; then I began to sing it. Then I wrote a song called "Empty Me." That moment of self-control was one of the greatest moments of the whole fast. I sang that song for years. I treasure it so much. It will forever be in my heart. You see, through this situation, God was teaching me to love Him above all else, and He was chiseling my character through self-control! God is so good, I love it when He teaches me through real-life experiences like that. He is awesome!

GOD IS SPEAKING!

Something I realize has been of great benefit to me through the years is this: During a fast, I journal and write down scriptures that minister to me every day. Because of my journaling, I can look back and see that there are very few days when I say that I really sense God's presence during a 40-day fast. There are probably four to six days in the entire 40 days of fasting when I really sense God's presence. Of course, when I do sense His manifested presence, it always strengthens me and helps me finish the fast.

I once asked the Lord why at times it feels like a desert in the midst of fasting. I thought I would feel God's presence every day—that I'd feel like I could walk on water! But, honestly, the opposite is true. Although there is grace and supernatural strength that comes on me, there are very few days when I experience a tangible encounter with God. I asked the Lord why it feels this way, and He replied to me, "Even in a desert, there is water! You just have to dig for it."

Then it hit me: If I really want to feel His presence, I just have to dig deeper. My devotion and time spent with God must increase if I want to encounter God.

This is very revealing! It's a test of your character! If you are fasting to get a feeling, you will not make it. This is a test of your commitment. Are you fasting because of a feeling, or are you fasting to bless God's heart, whether you feel anything or not?

Here is the deal: God is actually speaking to you every day. You feel His presence every day, but after a while, you get acclimated or used to it. It becomes normal to you. To sense more of Him; you need to lean into Him more and yield up more of yourself to Him.

The same is true when we get saved. We hear a message; our hearts are stirred. Tears roll down our faces, and we have an encounter with God like never before. As time goes by, we mature in the Lord, and that same message does not bless us as much. Why? Because that message was milk. We have matured, and now we need solid food.

I have experienced days in a fast when I press in and feel nothing. I have also experienced times when I press in, and a new revelation of God's Word and character opens up to me.

Regardless of what you feel, always keep pressing in to God, and He will give you understanding and direction to pursue. The key is to follow through. I promise—God will be faithful to you!

On the other hand, I have noticed that the rewards of a fast are almost never during the fast; the rewards usually come after the fact. In coming out of a fast, I journal just as I do when I am in the fast. And I have to tell you, I have received more revelation coming out of a fast than I have during that fast. The rewards, songs, and blessings have almost always come afterward for me.

Here are several motivations to break a fast correctly.

1. God will continue to discipline your flesh and chisel your character after the fast.

2. God will speak to you more after a fast than during it.

3. Blessings will start to flow into your life.

4. As you break the fast correctly, God changes your lifestyle and eating habits.

In closing this point, the Bible says that we are to do everything unto the Lord. That means we are to fast as unto the Lord and break a fast as unto the Lord. We will see as we do this that blessing comes as a result of our obedience— and that blessing will completely outweigh the discipline and sacrifice required to get there.

MY PRAYER

Father, thank You for giving me wisdom in breaking a fast. My body is the temple of the Holy Spirit, and I only get one, so I will honor You with my body. I receive all correction and direction that You are giving me through Your Word. I will exercise self-discipline and, as a result, I know that my life will change. I receive change in my habits and in my spiritual life. I make a commitment that I will fast as unto the Lord and I will break a fast as unto the Lord. I will do everything in my life as unto the Lord. Even in the days when I don't feel anything, I know that Your presence is with me, giving me rest and strength. In the days when it feels dry as a desert, I know that You are my Wellspring of refreshment, and I will dig deeper into You. I acknowledge that You are speaking to me every single day. I will follow Your direction and instruction. In the name of Jesus, I pray. Amen.

CONCLUSION

FASTING IS A powerful weapon that I believe every believer should use. If Jesus started His ministry with fasting, how much more should you and I fast as the Lord leads us.

Some situations cannot be overcome without fasting. Jesus highlighted this point in Mark 9:29 when a father brought his demon-afflicted son to the disciples, but they could not cast the spirit out. Jesus said that kind would not come out except by fasting and praying.

Another scripture, Matthew 17:20, describes that same story, saying that if you have faith like a mustard seed you can move mountains. Both are true. There will be times you cannot overcome something unless you fast and pray. The "mustard seed" in your life that causes mountains to move can be the actual fasting and praying.

I personally do not believe I could have followed the Lord's instruction to move to the US if I had not fasted and prayed beforehand. My flesh would not have been sufficiently under subjection to withstand the pressure and the uncertainty of walking out that assignment. Fasting and prayer are vital tools to help propel believers into their destiny.

Fasting with prayer is mentioned frequently in the Old and in the New Testaments. Jesus told us how we are to conduct ourselves "when you fast" not "if" (*see* Matt. 6:16-17). Clearly, fasting has a place in fortifying our relationship with God.

The heart posture of a fast is so important. We fast not just to see miracles and breakthroughs, but to touch God's heart. We don't fast for God's hand but for His heart. Yet we know it's true that if we touch His heart, God's hand will move.

Fasting is not about getting from God; it is about giving to God. We tend to have a consumer mindset, but if we are to touch the heart of God when we come to Him in prayer, we must come with a heart to give, not to get. When God sees that heart posture, He is more than happy to bless you and to bring breakthrough, but your heart posture has to be right.

Just as an earthly father does not like it when his children spend time with him only to get a gift, our Heavenly Father does not enjoy it when our relationship with Him is focused entirely on what we want to get from Him. He tolerates it and He will show mercy in the process, but if you want to go to the next level in your relationship with the Lord, you must fast to give and not to get. This is a powerful revelation.

Part of that heart posture is knowing that as you fast you do not move God, but fasting positions you to hear God's voice and aligns you with your true calling. As you take this heart posture you will hear God's voice more clearly than ever before. Fasting causes all of the other voices to be drowned out so that you can hear His voice and are strengthened to follow through with what He directs you to do.

Through it all, fasting and praying causes you to rise to new levels of relationship with God. It will transform your heart and change the way you view God and yourself. As you fast, you will realize that such power is a reality. As God continues to work on your character, you will feel Romans 8:11 become your daily experience: The same power and spirit that resurrected Christ from the dead is on the inside of you.

Fasting and praying will cause you to recognize and walk in the power of God that is already inside you. That mighty power within you will strengthen your relationship with the Lord and make you a mighty force against the enemy!

I believe every believer should fast and pray! It is foolish to ignore these great weapons in our spiritual arsenal. So let's use every weapon that God has given us so we can dismantle the devil's tactics and defeat him in the name of Jesus, every time!

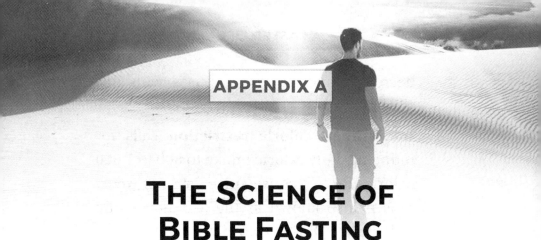

THE SCIENCE OF BIBLE FASTING

Popular Fasting Methods of Today

To have a better understanding of the science of fasting, here is a quick primer of popular fasting methods. There are three methods that are currently being promoted today in nutrition and science to lose weight and to obtain better health, increased longevity, and healing from illness. The award-winning science newsletter ENDPOINTS from Elysium Health covers all three.

1. **Time-restricted feeding** is the practice of limiting calorie intake to a certain time period, usually between 8 and 12 hours per day. It is based on the fact that our body has a clock in our colon, kidney, and liver, and it is beneficial to stay in sync with that internal clock. To simplify, according to this method you can only eat during an 8- to 12-hour period each day. Studies show that obesity

decreases and fitness increases with this method.

2. **Intermittent calorie restriction** calls for reducing daily caloric intake to 800 to 1,000 calories for two consecutive days per week. This is also known as the 5-2 diet or the 2-day diet. During two days of the week, you limit your caloric intake to 800 to 1000 calories. Studies show that it helps to take off weight and prevent chronic diseases. For normal, healthy people, the benefits of this particular practice are uncertain.

3. **Periodic fasting** requires limiting caloric intake for between three and five days, such that cells deplete glycogen stores and begin ketogenesis. During this fasting, bad cells are destroyed and replaced with rejuvenated cells with improved cognitive performance and decreased risk factors/biomarkers for aging, diabetes, and cardiovascular disease. Ketosis or Keto diet has been used since the 1920 to help epilepsy patients.

Any of the above fasting methods of periodic/Keto, inter-mittent, or time-restrictive fasting can improve your health and aid in weight loss.

Research and study the benefits of the science of fasting to understand more fully the keys of fasting that the Body of Christ needs to embrace.

Always consult a doctor when making a radical change in your diet or preparing to fast.

Combine the health and spiritual principles with the leading of the Holy Spirit for dynamic results!

Awaken to understand the power in a revival of the gift of fasting.

The different types of fasts acknowledged in the Bible are:

1. Vegetables and fruits—The Daniel Fast

2. Water and liquids only—The Nehemiah Fast

3. No food or drink—The Dry Fast

Never attempt any long fast if you haven't:

- Heard from God
- Established a right heart motive
- Consulted your doctor

THE DANIEL FAST

This fast consists of fruits, vegetables, and only water. Here is a guide of permitted foods.

The Daniel Fast Food List

- All fruit: fresh, frozen, dried, juiced, or canned.
- All vegetables: fresh, frozen, dried, juiced, or canned.
- All whole grains: amaranth, barley, brown rice, oats, quinoa, millet, and whole wheat.

- All nuts and seeds: almonds, cashews, macadamia nuts, peanuts, pecans, pine nuts, walnuts, pumpkin seeds, sesame seeds, and sunflower seeds; unsweetened almond milk. Nut butters are also included.

- All legumes: canned or dried; black beans, black-eyed peas, cannellini beans, garbanzo beans (chickpeas), great northern beans, kidney beans, lentils, pinto beans, and split peas.

- All quality oils: avocado, coconut, grapeseed, olive, peanut, sesame, and walnut.

- Beverages: distilled water, filtered water, and spring water.

The Daniel Fast has been adopted as a diet and many have benefited from it to gain back health. That's a good thing because in our Western culture we are generally not eating healthy and tend to have poor nutritional habits. High fat, high sugar, high caloric eating is hurting your body. Gluttony and other fleshly appetites are a hindrance spiritually as they push to rule and silence your spirit. Many are believing for healing when what they need is simply to change what they eat. You will find that by bringing your body into subjection regarding the simple matter of what and how you eat, you will be more sensitive to the to the spirit of God because you have required the flesh to stay under the control of your spirit. Additionally, making good dietary choices will guide you into physical well-being.

RESOURCES

Books

- *Fasting* by Jentezen Franklin
- *The Hidden Power of Fasting and Praying* by Dr. Mahesh Chavda
- *The Complete Guide to Fasting: Heal Your Body Through Intermittent, Alternate-Day, and Extended Fasting* by Dr. Jason Fung

About Philip Renner

Philip Renner is a missionary, author, worship leader, speaker, revivalist, and award-winning songwriter who has been given a mandate from the Lord to brand the land by leading worship in capitols and city halls across America. His media appearances include *TBN Praise, Lesea TV Harvest Show, Worship with Andy Chrisman, Atlanta Live TV, Cross Rhythms* UK, *TBN* UK, and *Premier Christian Radio* UK. Philip has also been featured in *CCM Magazine* and the *Tulsa World*. For more information, visit philiprenner.com.

OUR VISION

Proclaiming the truth and the power of the Gospel of Jesus Christ with excellence. Challenging Christians to live victoriously, grow spiritually, know God intimately.

Connect with us on

Facebook @ **HarrisonHousePublishers**

and Instagram @ **HarrisonHousePublishing**

so you can stay up to date with news about our books and our authors.

Visit us at **www.harrisonhouse.com** for a complete product listing as well as monthly specials for wholesale distribution.